My Teacher Rides a Harley

Enhancing K-5 Literacy through Songwriting

BY GARY DULABAUM

Illustrated by Michael Tonn

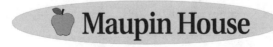

Maupin House

My Teacher Rides a Harley:
Enhancing K-5 Literacy through Songwriting

© 2003 Gary Dulabaum
All Rights Reserved

Cover Art: *Michael Tonn*
Cover and Layout Design: *Maria Messenger*
Edited by: *Mark Devish*

Library of Congress Cataloging-in-Publication Data

Dulabaum, Gary, 1955-
  My teacher rides a Harley : enhancing K-5 literacy through songwriting
/ by Gary Dulabaum.
      p. cm.
Includes bibliographical references (p.).
  ISBN 0-929895-56-8 (paperback, with music CD)
  1. Music in education. 2. Children's songs. 3. English
language--Study and teaching (Elementary) 4. Education,
Elementary--Activity programs. I. Title.
  MT1.D83 2003
  372.87--dc21
                                                    2003002288

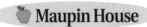 **Maupin House**

Maupin House Publishing, Inc.
PO Box 90148 • Gainesville, FL 32607
1-800-524-0634 • 352-373-5588 • 352-373-5546 (fax)
www.maupinhouse.com • info@maupinhouse.com

Publishing Professional Resources that Improve Classroom Performance

Table of Contents

Acknowledgements

I have always believed that I really don't have an original idea in my body, but that I am indeed like all good teachers: I steal, borrow, and learn from everybody I meet. I am like a human sponge. Of course, I do not try to be the people I learn from, and I certainly cannot do things exactly the way they do. I have my own individual stamp based on my skills that I have been developing and honing for quite a few years.

I have learned from so many people down through the years that I could not possibly name them all. But there are some that I do need to mention who have offered guidance, friendship, viewpoints, resources, great tunes, and above all, inspiration. So here I want to acknowledge and thank you who have inspired, motivated, listened to, shared, nudged, helped, challenged, and smiled at me during my 25 years of being an educator, songwriter, comedian, musician, and entertainer. It's been a fun journey and I am so happy that you folks have joined me for all or parts of the journey.

Dr. Stan Steiner: Your knowledge of children's literature is amazing, to say the least. I thank you from the bottom of my heart for all of your thoughts, ideas, and suggestions regarding my using music as a teaching tool. Your enthusiasm and support of my work has meant so much to me. I look forward to more inspiring late night walks, Stan.

Roseine Church: What can I say except thank you for taking a chance on me 12 years ago and bringing me to your wonderful Wyoming Whole Language Conference. Thank you for sharing all of your knowledge of books and reading and for introducing me to so many people.

Julie Agard: My friend who always wears a great smile. Thanks for introducing me to Nebraska!!!! You inspire me with your ability to make dreams come true and learning fun. Your energy level is amazing!!! Thank you!!!!

Jayne Cox: My good friend who really cares about children—all children—and the quality of education they receive. I remember when we first met: I knew from that moment you were someone special.

Marvia Boettcher and Joyce Hinman: thank you, folks, for all of your support and great times. Joyce, thank you for teaching me how to be flexible and cheerful. Marvia, you are the librarian that I always wanted.

Thank you also to Dr. Bob Wortman, an incredible educator who offered in my early days (and who continues to offer today) so many kind words. You are an inspiration to me and a good friend.

To all the great staff at Zaleski School in Zaleski, Ohio: you folks know how to teach and make kids believe in themselves. Thank you!!!

And thank you to all the kids in schools around the country who touch my heart and creativity every day. Your laughs and smiles are the best gifts and payments that I could ask for. You make what I do make sense.

Thank you to all of the great musicians and songwriters I have written with, sung with, and performed with through the years. Here's to more great musical times.

A big thanks to Brod Bagert for his writing on "Pages From The Past" and "My Teacher Rides A Harley."

Thank you to my mom and dad, Jackie and Marion Dulabaum. Mom, thanks for passing your great memory skills on to me and for always being such a great listener. You'll never know how much it meant to me that every time I played "Go Tell Aunt Rhody" on the banjo you found something positive to say about my playing. And you never said the same thing twice!!! Dad, what can I say, you are my favorite musician to tour with, and I love it that your amp dwarfs mine. That's how life should be. Dad, thank you also for the great phrase, "If you're too old to shake it, just turn it now and then." May we play many, many more tunes.

And finally to my favorite person, my wife Anne-Marie: thank you for helping me reach for the stars, think and act from the heart, and know what my true purpose is. Without you and your love and encouragement...well, I'd be singing a different tune.

CHAPTER ONE

Where It All Began:
The Spooky Old School on the Hill

My face was pushed up against the glass and my younger siblings refused to quit breathing (although I had asked nicely), so the fogged-up windows kept getting foggier and foggier. I tried to wipe a spot clear. People referred to the spooky old building on the hill as "*the* elementary school," like it was the only one in the world, and that fascinated me. Sure, the kids I could see on the playground *seemed* to be having a good time, but who could really tell from the back seat of a Chevy with fogged-up windows?

I had an older brother already attending the creepy old brick school, so I had heard all the rumors, both good and bad. There was one about kids that got locked in the basement for days on end, and one about teachers so mean they could scare your hair white, and one about the origins of the cafeteria food that I'd rather not repeat. I believed that all of my brother's stories were true, but still I thought school might not be too bad—if only I could avoid the Hitler-ish principal who constantly roamed the hallways looking for kids to make miserable. Rumor had it that he could make it so that problem kids never existed at all, and looking back on it, I guess he was a visionary when it came to the problem of school overcrowding—sometimes, students just disappeared. To this day, I still try to avoid being alone in school hallways (and eating cafeteria food).

Thankfully, my brother had also shared with me the joys of being a student: you saw your friends every day, you got your

1

own desk, and you were able to sharpen your pencil whenever you wanted. I was fascinated by pencils and their sharpeners, and a real industrial type, stuck-on-the-wall pencil sharpener was something I had dreamed about. (I didn't realize until later that you had to be able to write to use the pencil sharpener.)

Yes, I loved school—until I started attending. Playing school with my brothers and sisters in my parent's basement had been fun. We had real books, desk-like chairs, and did writing and a few other subjects (at least we thought they were subjects). My sisters (who usually played the teachers) were mean and unreasonable, but they seemed to care about me and about the lessons they were trying to teach. I guess their angry attitudes and physical punishments were good practice: when I started school for real, teaching was still a contact sport, and my real teachers turned out to be much worse.

I will never forget my first day of school. After years of waiting and anticipation, I finally made the trip up the hill for myself. And then, within minutes of stepping into that spooky old brick building on the hill, my excitement for school disappeared.

In general, school ended up not being a whole lot of fun for me. It seemed too disconnected and fragmentary, each subject quarantined off by itself, as if each was sterile and in danger of being contaminated by the others. None of the subjects were enjoyable. I remember coming to school in the morning anxious to see my friends. But once class started the joy of being there was gone.

I started school back in the good ole days of the early 1960s. Slide rules and big hair were still in fashion, there were no computers, and the spooky old school buildings smelled ancient and well worn, like your grandma's house but not as nice. All of the teachers looked old. (I suspected many of them had been teaching since the 1800s.) I see my early school pictures and I think that even I look old in a weary sort of way. I think it was the influence of those spooky buildings—they made everything old before their time.

My first teacher (who shall remain nameless—I am not famous or successful enough to handle a lawsuit) didn't seem all that excited to see me. She told me that I was the third, fourth or maybe even fifth Dulabaum that she had taught, and from the way she was looking at me, I wondered what they had done to her.

She was wearing a plaid button-down dress, dark colors, and prehistoric black pumps that clumped firmly on the floor when she walked towards me. She was very tall and on the massive side. Of course, she looked old (like I said, everything in that school looked old) and a bit on the tight side (no funny business welcome here, thank you very much).

In reality, she may not have been taller than five feet two in her pumps, but she seemed like a giant towering over me. I was terrified and began to cry. I cried all day that first day, and then every day for the next six weeks. My crying bothered my teacher, and she was strict with me from the get-go, making me miss recess and be late for lunch, and finally resorting to calling me a few choice names for good measure. I don't ever remember her ever being very comforting—just big and bothered.

Eventually, I stopped crying every day, and school became routine. I rode the bus with my friends, with the driver keeping one eye on the road and one eye out for misbehavior. When we got to school, the driver unloaded us row by row, skipping all the rows with delinquent and/or disorderly riders (these would be spirited away for the scolding of their young lives during a meeting with the Hitler-ish principal). Once inside, we headed right to our classrooms, with no lolligagging around. Our teachers usually greeted us in a cordial but formal manner and then we all kind of talked around each other before settling into our desks.

We'd start class some time after eight o'clock and do something that resembled science for about 40 to 45 minutes. Then we'd get up, go to the bathroom, and walk around until the science was completely out of our heads. Then maybe we'd do arithmetic, or spelling, or some fill-in-the-blank worksheets on subjects and verbs. It was like our science lesson had never really happened: there was no connection between the subjects, and it was never obvious (it was never made obvious) that the writing worksheets the teacher handed out could *ever* have anything to do with science, or math, or even reading.

In fact, the only subjects I can recall ever being done together were reading and detention. (I guess I had a little bit of trouble with authority at an early age: I was not a bad kid, but once I figured out that school was not for me, I had trouble being a model citizen. I spent quite a bit of time in detention, and reading was often assigned as punishment.)

Before I began my formal education I really believed that I liked to read, write, and sing. Within days of finally getting to school I found out (according to my first teacher) that I could do none of the above.

I always felt that I was missing something that was going on in my classes—it was like I was always on the wrong page, even when I knew I wasn't. Most days I felt disconnected, gave the wrong answers (actually I think I had the right answers, but was asked the wrong questions), and felt the need to constantly look around the room—I was sure something else *had* to be going on.

I still remember reciting the alphabet as my teacher pointed her big stick (which doubled as discipline tool and enforcer), and thinking that the letters must have done something wrong, to be poked and shouted at by the teacher like that.

My home was musical and I never remember a time that I didn't like music. My dad was the first musician I ever remember seeing and hearing. I loved the enjoyment he got from singing and playing. I mistakenly thought school music would be fun. Instead, the first few years of school music were spent doing worksheets and listening to music that I had no interest in. How boring!

There seemed to be so much baggage getting in the way of my education that I lost interest in my three R's: Readin', 'Ritin' (not Ritalin), and Rhythm. I felt like I was drowning in a sea of busy work and boring subjects.

Every time we began a unit on something that I enjoyed, I would give silent thanks—finally, we were going to do something I could understand! But then, just when it felt like we were getting started, it would be over.

Let's say we were doing a unit on poetry. From what I remember, poetry was always done at the same time each year for about a week, and then it was gone. It was like a short, bitter season that my teachers dreaded and wished could be avoided. I'm sure if they could have given us shots to make us immune to it, we never would have done it at all. But during the week that poetry infected the class, we'd write something that resembled a poem, maybe do a revision or two, and then... well, that was it. We were finished.

Creative writing projects **always** came with a time limit, usually 40 to 50 minutes. We "finished" our writing, got a grade on it, then took it home to have our parents tape it to the refrigerator (there were no kitchen magnets then). And then it was over.

My penmanship was rough (it remains so today: I can't use traveler's checks because I can never write my name the same way twice). My reading skills were somewhat better but not great. I was not a model citizen. And I suspect that my teachers were right—I wasn't always trying as hard as I could. But I also suspect that if my teachers had been trying as hard as *they* could—if they had met me even a quarter-way—things would have been different. If I had been invited to enjoy my education, I think I would have.

Before I started school, I loved to read. Even though my skills were a long way from developed, reading opened up my imagination, and I loved the way I felt when enjoying a good story. However, mix a bit of stutter with books like *I like Bugs*, *A Bundle of Sticks*, and *Poof, Poof,* and you may get an idea of why reading in school was not always fun for me.

Reading time in my good ole days meant three reading groups: Group One was composed of the excellent to pretty doggone good readers, Group Two had the pretty good to pretty well emerged readers, and Group Three—the boys group—well, I guess we were the sub-mergent readers.

Reading time began each day with Group One. Those of us in Groups Two and Three, while not reading, were to keep our noses to our desks and our eyes on yet another worksheet.

Reading time began when the teacher would peel—with hands that had been mimeographed purple—worksheets from her fragrant stack and distribute them to those of us in Groups Two and Three. As Group One got settled in for their reading time, she would peer at us sternly and shout, "YOU ALL HAVE WORK TO DO!!!" Realizing that my completing the worksheet in the given amount of time was just not going to happen, I would lift my head and enjoy Group One's reading adventure. What an incredible skill, to be able to read. I was amazed and impressed by those classmates who could read like it was "nothin' doin'."

Group One read first every day. They were mostly girls with a few bright boys (who were no friends of mine). Group One's members zipped right through basal readers, poems, charts, chapter books—anything you wanted them to read, they could. Group One readers even brought books from home. They were obviously sucking up to the teacher.

Our teacher loved it.

Group One could offer summaries before they'd finished reading. They wouldn't leave out a fact, a scene, nothing! It was all there in their summaries. In fact, I believe they even included things the author could have written but didn't, and things that had maybe been edited out in New York.

Group One could read silently, or they could read out loud. They used their fingers to actually hold the book and turn the pages, not point at or underline words. Man, I was impressed. I knew we were talking pre-Mensa here. Plus, they had confidence. They had a reader's posture. They had voice. They actually understood what they read. They were the real deal, as far as I could tell.

It was obvious that the teacher favored her stars in Group One, and spent extra time with them. I think their lessons were often extended just because the teacher didn't want to spend her energy on the less-able groups.

Group Two read next. I actually knew some of the members in Group Two—it contained a roughly equal number of boys and girls, and their reading abilities were good, but not great in that Group One way.

You could tell which group was reading by the tone of the language that the teacher used. Her encouragements and compliments disappeared as soon as Group One yielded the floor. Group Two was more than likely given a steady diet of critiques: "Start at the left side." "Stop. You know better than that." "Slow down." "Stop. Take a breath." "Stop! Begin that line again." "Read that again, with feeling, now. It sounds like you're reading a worksheet." "Stop!! Sound it out." "Stop, I tell you, STOP!!!" That final "STOP" meant that she could no longer tolerate Group Two's skills.

Group Two had some fine readers amongst them, but the teacher's haranguing seemed to totally exhaust them by the time their reading out loud time was done. Of course, they really weren't done with reading time: recall and summaries always followed reading out loud. Most Group Two members knew that a "summary" was not the opposite of a "wintery," and they did a good job remembering the most important events and characters. But there were always some that had to be prodded.

For example, picture this one fine sunny morning. Group Two has just finished reading "Paul Revere's Ride" by Henry Wadsworth Longfellow. They are fatigued, slumping in their little wooden chairs. The teacher has been shaking her head and shouting "STOP!!!" a lot. It is clear she wants recall and summary to go better than reading out loud.

However, it is also clear that she has a bit of revenge on her mind as well. A boy I'll call Bernie had found "Paul Revere's Ride" to be an irresistible target and had cracked jokes about Paul and his horse all through the reading. (Bernie had a special talent—not only could he read, he could read the instructions on a worksheet or the directions in our spelling book in a way that made them sound dirty. It was a well developed and much appreciated skill.)

The teacher looks the group over slowly, making sure that everyone has a moment where they think they're going to get picked. I could tell she was going to go after Bernie, but she makes a show of it, scanning every face in the group. Finally she walks over and stands right in front of Bernie's desk. "What was this poem about?" she asks.

"It's about a guy," Bernie says. I admired his poise under pressure.

"Guy? What guy? You'll have to do better than that," the teacher said (she was great at giving life-threatening cues).

Bernie says, "The guy in the story."

8

The teacher's face begins to glow a bit. "Oh, brother," she says. "I could be grooming poodles for a living." How Bernie could hold a neutral face—perfectly innocent, no hint of fear, no show of disrespect—was beyond me. "What was 'the guy's' name?" the teacher finally says to him, frustration turning the words into sneers.

Bernie makes a show of thinking hard—moving his eyebrows around, licking his lips, grinding a knuckle into his forehead. "Mmmmmm," he says. "Oh, yeah. It was Paul."

"What was Paul's last name, please?" You could hear the pressure building up behind her voice, and I wondered how long it would take before she would explode.

Bernie pauses for a second, and I suspect that he was judging how far he could push it. In what I'm sure was a learning experience for him, Bernie found one of the boundaries on our teacher's patience (and I use that word loosely). "Why?" he asks. "Didn't *you* read the poem?"

There is a moment when the room is washed by peals of laughter (although the kids from Group One only look annoyed), but when the teacher reaches down and grabs Bernie by the back of his neck there is only silence. She holds him in the "death grip," her thumb and forefinger pinched together in the middle of his shoulders, and Bernie's body is suddenly useless, his eyes popping open and bugging out wide.

Finally it was time for Group Three, the boys' group (which did have one unfortunate girl stuck right in the middle), to read. I don't want to generalize, but most of Group Three's members had little use or understanding of the written word. This is the group that I called home. We had kids who stuttered, kids with major speech problems, kids who drooled and opened their mouths and said nothing, and kids now known as cultural orphans. These kids, the cultural orphans, had not been read to, sung to, and probably had never been to a library. We had one group member who would sit in his little wooden chair and raise his hand and keep it up. If he was called on, which was rarely, he would always ask the same question: "What am I doing here?" I remember thinking it was a pretty good question.

The teacher was enthusiastic about Group One, critical of Group Two, and resigned to her duty with Group Three. If there was time after Groups One and Two had read, and if the teacher was feeling up to it, Group Three got a chance.

At some point, the teacher had had the great idea to put all of the Group Three readers in a circle so that we could watch—and perhaps model for—each other. After all, it is quite hard to get stutterers to stutter in time. So Group Three's reading time always started with the spectacle of our moving our desks into a circle while the members of the other two groups watched. And then we'd sit there, staring, watching each other move around, contorting our faces, trying to get our lips to find a rhythm to carry us through.

Embarrassed in unison, Group Three never felt like it was making progress. Instead of the steady stream of critiques offered to Group Two, our teacher gave us a mortified silence. She hardly seemed to be listening at all.

But I guess we got better, if slowly. I did, after all, finally learn to read. However, I don't remember any Group Three member saying, "Boy, I can't wait to get home and read tonight!" We were too tired.

A reading certificate given to me in 1964 states that I read all sorts of books at school—*Story of Little Big, Poof, Poof, We Like Bugs, A Bundle of Sticks,* and *Flagon the Dragon* among them—but really I only remember the Alice and Jerry series.

Yes, Alice and Jerry, that great basal series that many readers read as young students. As reading material, the books left a lot to be desired, but as props to hold the windows open, they were great. Some of you may be more familiar with the Dick and Jane series, but in my school, it was Alice and Jerry. It doesn't really matter, because I believe they are more or less the same: books going nowhere fast.

The Alice and Jerry series (as with the Dick and Jane) is a mild basal soap opera starring—who else?—Alice and Jerry. They are a brother and sister who appear to be latch-key kids (they might even be independent orphans—I don't remember ever meeting their parents in the stories) with only two friends: Mr. Carl and Jip the dog. Mr. Carl is an old man who lives next door. He appears to have no adult friends and shares a big ole house with a parrot (I'm not sure if the parrot had a name—even if it did, I don't see how it would have improved the story). Mr. Carl seems to keep a keen eye on Alice and Jerry and is always inviting them over to his house. Social workers and child psychologists of today would frown on this close, unsupervised relationship for sure. Jip the dog? Well, he runs, and he also acts as if he understands language. Of course, how hard is "Run, Jip, run!" to figure out?

I do remember that reading-time mantra: "Run, Jip, run. Here comes Alice and Jerry." Even though I wasn't much of a reader, I knew right away that Alice and Jerry were going nowhere fast. If these characters were real people they would have been in therapy for sure. Actually, I think therapy would have helped the story immensely. For me, and for the characters in the book.

One thing I will say in support of my early reading days: between all three reading groups we did quite a bit of reading out loud, which was somewhat enjoyable. And I don't believe I ever really cried during reading time. I saved my crying for early morning settling-in, and for math.

Despite my struggles with reading, writing, and school in general, I somewhere along the line realized that my teachers were probably doing the best they could. Somewhere deep in their hearts they believed that the three reading groups and books like the Alice and Jerry series were some day going to be a help to me in some way. I cannot fault my teachers for this. But I do have to say that teaching needs to be more about developing the students as whole people, and that reading and writing are not just important for good test scores, but so that each and every student will be able to creatively and clearly communicate throughout their lives.

Even though school did little to encourage me as a lover of books or writing, I was able to find that place in my heart that let me know that I was going to be a reader, a writer, and a communicator for life. It was just going to take some time. My journey, of course, turned out to be quite different from my classmates'. Somewhere along the line I ran into adults (teachers and non-teachers) who understood how I learned and what interested me (books and writing). Today I read more books (of all kinds) than you can shake a stick at, and I write every day.

So, in closing this section I would ask all of you to remember that teaching is a commitment to guide today's youth on a lifelong journey of learning. That journey will include many successes and failures—and you have to remember that no matter how hard you try, you may not be able to reach every student.

But do know that you can help your students recognize and develop their own personal learning styles. Creativity is an important tool for helping folks find their own personal learning process and style, and that is why I believe helping people connect with their own personal creativity is so important.

As a teacher, don't be afraid to take risks. Start the morning or after-lunch sessions with stories about your life as a kid who loved books and who loved to write. Share who you are now, and what you are doing as an adult to continue growing in your own learning process. Be humorous, be serious, be whatever you need to be at that moment, but always be who you really are. Be sincere.

After a certain age students really are half responsible for their learning and education. You have to keep it interesting, but you also have to let them know that you are counting on them to participate, to contribute, and to speak up. But always make it clear that they have to compromise as needed, that they need to be individuals who can also be team players. Demonstrate through activities that build community that each person in the room is a small but significant part of the world. We all belong—we just need to build awareness of our differences and similarities.

There are lots of ways to bring creativity into your classroom. Write a class song. Start each morning with instrumental music to set the classroom mood. Ask your students to bring in a poem to share with the class. For in-service training have each teacher bring in a favorite song, poem, or passage. Make a tape of each teacher reading what they brought in. Brainstorm curriculum ideas for each piece. Have those ideas put on a disk, a paper, or a booklet and distribute them (with a copy of the tape) to every teacher in the school. Look at all of the resources you can come up with as a staff. As a bonus, notice how great a way (one of many) sharing literature is to bring the staff together.

Remember, it does matter how you approach things. If you don't have any interest in what you are teaching, I doubt your students will either. Find what you love, your passions, and find a way to teach what you need to teach in a way that excites you as well as your students. If your main teaching tool is drama, use drama whenever you can. If it's music, use song. Use everything you can get a hold of. Remember, if you have more than one student, you'll have more than one learning style. Above all, remember that you as a teacher are important. Don't be fooled by TV sitcoms that show teachers as bumbling idiots and students as smart-mouthed kids.

Rise to the challenge. Go for it. It's up to you. Bring your class alive. It's up to you.

> "Few people in today's society have as powerful an influence over youngsters as do the singers of songs. When the words from songs your students know are used as reading material, the language experience is deepened."

> –Mimi Brodsky Chenfeld, *Teaching Language Arts Creatively*

CHAPTER TWO

It's Instrumental

Music—as a vehicle of expression and learning—can be instrumental to making personal connections with the what-makes-things-tick. It's a great way to challenge yourself. Risk-taking in music is safe and productive.

Thanks in part to my connection to songwriting, I have gone from being a young, frightened child who hated school so bad that he cried every day for weeks to being an adult who just can't learn enough. This is true. If I didn't have to sleep, I wouldn't. I'd spend my time reading, writing, researching, exploring, and just plain learning everything I could. I am a hands-on type of person who loves the abstract, the humor of things: more than anything, I want to know how everything relates to me, to my life.

I need to experience life taking safe risks in order to challenge myself every day. (If I feel the need to compete with anybody, it is with myself—I try to do better.) I believe I have been this way my whole life, even if I couldn't express it in words way back then.

In a perfect world (according to my own biased but I believe logical opinion), language arts instruction would include reading, writing, music, movement, drama, dance, performance poetry, the visual arts, and the study of rhythm and how rhythm affects and relates to language. These subjects are all celebrations of language and are the true tools that people need to be able to clearly and creatively communicate throughout their lives.

In my perfect world, every school would not have one music teacher, but perhaps four or five: one to teach vocal instrumentation, one to teach band, one to help in the language arts department, and two others to work with teachers in the other curriculum areas.

In this perfect world, music would be integrated into the whole curriculum. Personal creativity, emotional development, self-expression, good decision making, and the development of the whole child/student would be just as important as any test score.

The changes needed in our educational system—the changes needed to bring about this perfect world—may not happen in any of our lifetimes. That's too bad. In the meantime, there *are* activities that can be brought to the classroom that will interest, inspire, and motivate your students to learn, express, and create.

I have been to schools of every kind, all across the United States, and wherever I go I find that students love to write songs. Music helps bring tone and color to a piece of writing, which helps students convey emotion with their words. Since students usually hear and react to the beat before they do the words, a hypnotic, finger-and-foot tapping beat also makes it easier for them to connect with the writing.

If you really want to know how much knowledge a student has on a subject, have them write a song about it. Songwriting can be used with creative or expository writing. I just don't know why more teachers aren't using song lyrics written by famous songwriters—as well as songs and poems written by their own students—for classroom reading materials.

The only limits you may face when writing songs with students are your own fears and lack of confidence. Hopefully, this book will help give you the tools and resources you need to find your creative comfort zone.

KINDERGARTEN KARAOKE

I have presented Kindergarten Karaoke (thank you to writer Roland Smith for the cool name) at hundreds of schools across the nation. Whenever I present it, it usually goes something like this:

I am at a school that has many students (across all grade levels) who are having trouble reading and writing. I am there to lead them in a songwriting workshop. They get excited about the activity, learn the basic songwriting process, participate in writing and re-writing sessions, and *voila!* we have songs from every class that we share during a school-wide assembly at the end of my visit.

After we have presented all the class songs to the assembly, I set up a sound system in the gym, with a couple of microphones on stands, two huge speakers, a mixer, and a boom box for playing the CDs that the students have brought in. I have a sign-up area and have the kids sign up to sing. They can either sing along with a CD, have me and some other musicians back them up, or they can sing pure and simple *a cappella*. It's up to them.

I ask each group (either as they sign up or as they get ready to sing), "Is the language in this song appropriate for school?" Unfortunately, you do need to ask something like this, to make sure the song doesn't contain questionable material. Being surprised by offensive content in front of an assembly is no fun. I used to ask, "Can you sing it in front of your parents?" but that doesn't work anymore. The kids are almost always 100% honest about the lyrical content and when a school does Kindergarten Karaoke on a regular basis the students will police themselves.

Anyhow, as each student (or group of students) takes center stage and gets behind the mic, we cue up their CD and then say,

"You're on." The assembly listens respectfully for the title of the CD and any other comments the singers have, like what the tune means or says to them. But as soon as the students on stage start singing, the students in the audience begin singing along. Not just one or two of them, but *almost all* of them. And they seem to know every word of the song. Amazingly, they do this for every singer or group of singers. They sing along with *every* song. Plus, if a group has the dance and movements to go with their song, the students all get up, and all of them seem to know every step.

I'm talking *a lot* of songs here, a lot of words—and they seem to know the proper emotion and tone to go with each line's meaning. Do all of these students have copies of every one of these CDs? Do they all have copies of the lyrics? I don't think so. They have learned these words from listening to the songs they hear (on the radio, on TV, at their friends' houses) over and over and over again—so many times that the language has become their own. Imagine children responding like this to something you are trying to teach them. It can happen, with every one of your students.

You may question your own creative skills as an artist, dancer, or singer—after all, the world isn't perfect yet. Does this mean you should forget the creative teaching and stick to teaching "in the box"? Absolutely not. The way to get good at songwriting, just like getting good at anything else, is by doing it. (That is the reason for this book, which has taken me forever to complete.) I have worked with thousands of teachers who feel they have no musical or songwriting skills and do not know where to begin. After thousands of school visits, teacher in-services, and conference workshops, I have put together some ideas about songwriting, and a basic songwriting process that I actually use on a daily basis in my workshops, school programs, and my own personal writing. I can honestly say this songwriting process works, is not hard to do, and makes it possible to take your songwriting as far as you want. The sky's the limit when it comes to how you use songwriting in your classroom.

This book not only has the process, it also has ideas on songwriting, tools and equipment you'll need for songwriting, some songwriting resources, and a list of common songs that can be used for piggybacking your new words (it is much easier to write to an established tune because then you are working with a familiar pattern). However, as their songwriting skills evolve, many teachers begin making up their own tunes. You can build your confidence level by working on some songs by yourself, before you begin writing with your students.

The power of songwriting extends beyond the classroom. It is an activity that can shape many areas of your students' lives. Creativity is a tool that I feel everyone—young, old, teacher, student— should have in their arsenal of ways to deal with the world.

I feel I have a responsibility as a writer and a performer to offer children programs that they can actively be involved in, that help them connect with their own personal creativity, and that offer a positive, yet not preachy, message. I hope to touch their hearts *and* stimulate their imaginations.

I have visited several schools in order to lead songwriting workshops on drug prevention and peer mediation. During the course of these week-long visits we write some incredible songs about making good decisions, peer mediation, and saying no to drugs. We also write songs about topics that are important to the students and that help them feel good about who they are.

Creativity has been a great prevention tool for me. I would not want to do anything that might harm my thinking capacity (I need all the help I can get). But it goes much deeper than that. Creativity allows me to express myself clearly. I believe that when a person can clearly and creatively communicate they are better able to tackle problems and address issues without resorting to more destructive means (like drugs or fighting). I believe that creative, arts-based teaching levels the playing field for all students. I may seem naïve, but I have seen that creativity works with all kids, including those on the fringe.

During my prevention workshops, we write about topics that cover many themes: family, friends, music, food, TV shows, school, history, responsible decision making, etc. No matter what we choose to write about, before we begin we always hold discussions on how to approach the topic, what the message we are trying to convey is, and who it is that we are trying to write for. These pre-writing discussions are an important part of the songwriting process, and offer the opportunity to encourage students to think creatively about the topic at hand, and about life in general.

Creativity comes from the heart, requires thinking before acting (especially when using the imagination), and is something that can be shared with peers. When students share the songs they have written, it is not unusual for comments such as, "Wow, I can really relate to that," or "You know, I have felt that same way before" to come up. Receiving recognition and positive feedback from peers after sharing a song is an incredible boost to one's confidence that usually leads to an improved self-image.

All people can be creative. It's innate in all of us. However, sometimes we need other people to help us find and develop our own personal creativity. Being creative will change your whole life. You'll never be bored, and everything you do will reflect your creativity, including the ways you communicate. Drug and alcohol use, unsafe risks, and irresponsible decision making can dull your creativity, harm your body, and change the direction of your life. Creativity is a positive force, and once people experience its power firsthand, they will not want to harm it. Who would want to harm something that has a positive effect on their lives?

THE POWER OF COMMUNICATION

Teaching students how to clearly and creatively communicate is one of the goals I have as a teacher. When communication breaks down, problems occur. (Lack of communication can lead to daily problems like fighting, or having difficulties in school, and can blossom into life-long struggles with drugs or alcohol.) Much of my workshop time is spent teaching kids how to *say* (or more appropriately, *sing*) the things that they feel they need to share. However, since communication is a two-way process, I also spend time teaching kids how to listen to each other. Active listening is an important skill we all need to have: when students know that their audience won't be judging them, but instead will be offering suggestions, constructive feedback, and their own feelings on the matter, they will be more apt to share what's troubling them.

We can all learn from each other, and creative expression (like songwriting or poetry) presents a way for everyone—teachers and students—to open up and share their thoughts in a productive way. Students on the edge of trouble will almost always drop hints, but people need to be listening in order to hear them. People need to know that others care. They want to feel safe.

All students need the venue and the time to say what's on their minds. Including songwriting in your curriculum will allow your students to express themselves in a creative, safe way where they know they won't be judged. They will learn to take ownership for what they say and do, and to take responsibility for their actions and words. In short, teaching your students how to write songs will teach them that they belong in the world, and that they can say things that are important to people other than themselves.

Music is a powerful teaching tool. The rhythmic patterns of the lines and verses make words easy to learn, and the beat encourages students to find their own voices. Once you let your students know that they can create cool songs with cool beats to help them learn what they need to know, there will be a change in your classroom. And when your students have learned the power of creativity, they will always have a tool they can use to help them through the problems in their lives.

Songs—like books—are true celebrations of language. It is my hope that you'll find something interesting and useful in this book, and that you will come to realize the power of music and songwriting, and their true connection to the language arts.

Happy writing.

Young Authors

Young authors are we.
Learning a skill,
Creating such a thrill,
There is excitement in our classrooms.

Writing process.
What's your approach?
Think. Write. Discuss. Share.
Re-write!

Create!
Short stories and prose,
And poetry that flows,
From mind to pencil to paper.

We tinker with words,
Build phrases that amaze.
Edit!
Coming together like magic.

Ideas?
If we feel it,
We own it,
We don't fight it,
We just write it.

We research and write.
We edit and write.
Draft after draft,
Our goal is to write.

We create—we read,
We share—we listen.
Feedback—another draft.
Should I edit?
No, it's complete—I can feel it.

Young Author's Competition?
In the hall—on the wall,
People stop and read.
A crowd gathers,
I give a smile.
I wonder do they know I'm the author?

"Great job,"
My teacher says.
She's worked hard with me,
I know she's proud.

Back to work,
Young Authors meet
Relate your own experience.
We had stories to tell.
Our writings had a purpose.
We accepted the challenge – we created.

Yes, Young Authors are we,
Writing with such skill,
Creating such a thrill,
I believe our numbers are growing.

(1994)

I wrote this poem several years ago to celebrate the joy of writing
in school. The International Reading Association as an organization

has been very important to me in so many ways, both as an educator and as a writer. Their Young Author Events are pure joy. After attending, presenting, performing, and just listening in the audience at many of these events I was inspired one night to write this poem in honor of all young writers and teachers who support these writers.

I might add that I wrote this poem in my favorite writing place, above the clouds on a jet plane, 35,000 feet in the air. To me, writing just doesn't get much better than that.

CHAPTER THREE

Songwriting 101

Songwriting is a very personal activity. I don't believe there is a wrong or right way to do it (of course there are rules like grammar and punctuation so that people can understand what you have written, but you can still develop your own personal style). You just have to write, write and write some more, and write what feels right to you. Writing is a way to express, a way to deal with issues, and a way to keep a personal history.

Writing is where knowledge and imagination come together. I enjoy writing poems, stories, jokes, and essays, but songwriting is my favorite form of writing. As a songwriter who is also an educator, I decided I really needed to have goals to give me guidance and direction. Even though I strongly believe "just because it's fun" is reason enough, I recognized that I needed a purpose for songwriting in schools. So I designed the following goals.

MY GOALS

Keep the learning active and actively engage all students in their own personal learning.

Offer activities that challenge students, focus on the learning process, and help students connect with their own creativity. Goals and objectives are necessary for guidelines and structure, but they must be flexible. We really need to teach students to enthusiastically enjoy and use the learning process in their writing. When their focus is on the process instead of on an end product, the students have more room for successful outcomes.

As a songwriter, I love the learning process. I love the hunt for ideas, the work, and the excitement of the new song. I know that my Mom and Dad may be the only ones to really like 90% of what I write. But the other 10% will be great. And I always know that some of what I throw away can be recycled for other writing projects. The learning process keeps me from getting discouraged.

As writers, our goal is to write, draft after draft. Focusing on the process helps students clearly see that the more they write, the better writers they will become. Especially if, with their peers, they form a learning community. In my ideal community we all actively listen, create, express, share, and offer feedback.

Give all students their day(s) on center stage. It takes lots of nerve and confidence to get up and share something as personal as a song, poem, or story. It can seem like people are not only critiquing your work, but also you the writer. But when they are ready to, students need to share what they have written. Sharing with peers, and getting their feedback, is an important part of the learning process.

Prepare students to be respectful, responsive audiences who will share critiques that are meant to help each other improve. Let students know that they may disagree with their classmates' comments and criticisms, but that writers need to be good listeners and accept others' critiques of their topics and writing style. Make sure your students know that listening to audience feedback doesn't mean you have to agree or accept 100% of the suggestions, but that hearing good, positive feedback can do nothing but help you as a writer. If your critics are speaking from the heart and have really thought out their comments, you'll at least want to think about what they have said, as this could present options or angles you hadn't previously considered.

It's important to be aware of the audience you are writing for. Knowing, as you write, what you stand for as a writer, how much of your own personal opinions you wish to share, and what response you are looking for, will help when forming a response to your audience's comments. As your students are writing, they may want to ask themselves, "Is this something that my peers, students my age, from anywhere, can relate to and say 'Hey, that's happened to me,' or 'I know exactly what you are talking about.' Or will their response be something like 'I really have no idea what you are writing about'?"

ON FEEDBACK

As the teacher, you'll have lots of options for making sure your students have the opportunity to share their work with their classmates, and to encourage constructive feedback. Set up clear class rules, and make sure your students understand the guidelines for giving—and getting—feedback.

You might consider working with other teachers to set up opportunities for your students to share their work with other classes, or even with other grade levels. Maybe you could work with your principal to coordinate a special school-wide sharing assembly (like the ones we hold after my visits to schools). Think how cool it would be to arrange to do special visits with other schools or districts.

Giving Feedback

Writers like clear, constructive, sincere feedback. Encourage your students to really take the time to think about what they have just read or heard. Tell them to take notes and put thought into their comments. Make sure they can state, in plain words, what it is that they are trying to say. Tell them to avoid general feedback like "Yea, it was okay" or "your writing is good." Instead, they might suggest that the piece reminds them of another poem or song. Encourage them to state their reasons why. Tell them that they need to mention it if parts of the lyric or poem don't make sense to them, but remind them of how important it is for them to be supportive and clear.

Getting Feedback

When you are being critiqued, it's often hard not to take criticism personally. Tell your students that they must be good listeners when they are getting feedback. Remind them that their peers are there to help them become better writers, and that they need to know where their writing isn't working as well as they might hope. Being an open-minded listener is so critical here. Tell your students to accept criticism in the same light that they offer criticism when they are reading someone else's piece.

Here are some helpful hints to share with your students when they are looking for feedback, whether they are writing for school, for music lessons, or for any reason:

Put your writing in a folder, maybe accompanied by a tape of you reading it. Make sure your piece is properly titled, and that all multiple-page pieces are in order and include page numbers. Leave the folder in a place that friends and family members can get to it and borrow it.

You may want to **write a little blurb to accompany your writing**. Try to help the reader understand your feelings when you wrote it, what inspired you, and any other information that help sets up the piece, but doesn't totally give away what you are writing about. Let the reader/listener come to their own conclusions about what they are reading.

Let the person reading or listening to your writings know what you are looking for regarding feedback. Do you want a proof reader? Do you want general or more specific/descriptive feedback? Would you like to know the strong points, best lines, great phrases? How's the rhythm and flow? Would you like to know if audience could follow and understand your writing?

Would it be helpful to know if they think your writing is too personal to be universally understood?

Give the person critiquing your writings some time when you are not around so they can read, reread, and think about what you have written. Hopefully they will have enough time to put your writings aside for a day or so, and then come back and read them again. If you have let your reader/critic know what you are looking for regarding feedback this will help them. Encourage your readers to take notes so that they will be able to offer specific suggestions and comments.

Set up a time when your reader/critic is done to meet in a relaxed atmosphere where you can talk about the writings. **Have a list of questions prepared** to ask the reader about your writings: Is my writing style easy to read and follow? Am I too wordy? How is the plot and character development? How is my spelling? What were some lines from my writing that really caught your attention or that you thought were really good? Is this strong writing? Where are the weaknesses? Is the topic I have chosen to write about one that other readers can relate to? Does my writing hold your interest? Does my writing make sense to you?

The sky's the limit regarding questions that you can prepare for your critic/reader. Make sure that your questions will obtain the information that you are seeking. Encourage the reader to ask you any questions that they may have regarding use of a word, the opening line of a paragraph, plot and character development, etc. Make good use of your reader/critic and let them know that you sincerely appreciate their time and efforts.

Remember, often times writers want immediate feedback, even though they know it's at the wrong place or the wrong time. You might be tempted to walk up to a friend or classmate and hand them a piece of writing and say, "Please read this and tell me what you think," and then stand right there as they try to read.

There are times and occasions when this type of feedback can work, but usually it pressures readers to say the first thing that pops into their heads, which may be very disappointing to you, as it is not the meaningful feedback that you were looking for. In most cases, it is better to give the reader/critic time to do a good job and not put them on the spot.

To close, remember: "If we feel it, we own it. We don't fight it, we write it. Draft after draft our goal is to write."

Happy writing!

CHAPTER FOUR

The Material World

What types of equipment and tools do you need to write songs? Not many at all—a good imagination fed by great books, stories, and life experiences is all that you really need. But here is a partial list of some other items you may wish to have on hand.

For me the basics for songwriting are a pad of paper, a couple of pens, and a small cassette player with one blank tape. But there are lots of other useful songwriting materials. The following is a list of items I use and like to have with me when I am writing. This is not a complete list, and your list will probably have items like mine, and some things unique to you. Ask other writers for their recommendations on useful writing tools and resources. It can only help.

MATERIALS USEFUL FOR SONGWRITING

Dictionaries, including a Rhyming Dictionary: Great for having words at your fingertips, especially when you want and need to rhyme. Most rhyming dictionaries break words down by the rhyming or beginning vowel sounds, which is a big help for young writers.

Thesaurus: Synonyms and antonyms at your fingertips. Many common words as well as words you may never use. As a writer, words are where it's at. You need this book—it may be one of your best resources.

Metronome: Why a metronome? To help keep time. Like a click track in a recording studio (which gives musicians a steady beat to play along with), the metronome offers a solid, steady beat that you can write along with.

Try using rhythm and musical instruments while you're writing, either as accompaniment or for background highlighting. With instruments and your metronome, you can establish a smooth rhythmic beat that can put life into words that aren't working the way that you want them to. You may be inspired to rewrite and search for words that will convey the message you want to get across. Metronomes and rhythm instruments are great tools for editing wordy passages and rough edges.

The metronome is also useful in the classroom, because it produces a rhythm that emergent and struggling readers can read along to. The metronome can be adjusted to various beats and tempos that match your readers' ability and skill levels. Since you play music and sing along with a metronome, it makes perfect sense that you could read along with a metronome. Rhythm and flow are important reading skills and help make reading more enjoyable for the reader, at least from my experience. I have noticed that the more rhythmically the words flow, the easier it is for emergent and struggling readers to read and comprehend the piece.

Small notebook or spiral pad: Carry a writing pad at all times to write down interesting lines you hear or to record ideas that hit you at any time. Write down lines, phrases, ideas, and the starts of songs. You never know when something you hear or think about will start looking like a song.

Journal/notebook: I am constantly recycling ideas. They get dropped from one song and reappear in another. A journal makes a good place for long-term storage. Here's where you store the lines and verses you cut from your songs. As a writer, you will continually be going back to these for use in other songs.

Your journal might be the place where you keep all your drafts. Don't erase. Cross out so that you know where you have been and what you have already tried regarding phrases, words, sentences, endings, characters, etc.

Tape player: Something that will really help your writing is to record yourself reciting/reading your own compositions. Listen to the flow of your voice, your articulation, your phrasing, your style, speed, tone, and rhythm. What is your reaction when you play back your readings? Your first reaction may be that you don't like your voice, but once you get past that you'll probably notice wordy phrases, lines that give you problems, phrases that don't flow, etc. Actively listening to your interpretations of your compositions will help you in the revision process, and can point out where punctuation and breaths should be.

It will also help you develop a speaking voice that really promotes and showcases the way that you feel your writings should be.

A tape player is also good for recording lines and ideas as they come to you. Titles, words, phrases, opening lines, topics that you may encounter, read, hear or think about are easily captured. While writing, it is very easy to record the background and ideas behind why you chose a certain word, phrase, title, etc. You can document what inspired you to write on the subject, what message you want to convey with this writing, and ideas for revision. Tape players are must-have tools for writers.

Computers are okay to use, but only if you remember to save all versions/drafts. The issue here is that computers do not cross out, they delete. When a word, line, phrase, or verse is deleted, you may not remember it. Knowing what you tried in earlier drafts is important. Writers need to see where they have been. I put each new song that I start on its own disc so that I am able to store all changes, re-writes, revisions, thoughts, questions I had regarding lyrics, or ideas I have on the song.

As I'm writing, I print out a first draft and then dabble a bit by hand. I use the first draft until there are enough changes and I am ready for the next draft. Then I make the changes to the computer file and save the new draft under a different name. That way I have a record of each draft that I've worked on.

Pitch Pipe to help you find the key/pitch that is comfortable for you to sing in.

Musical instruments: guitar, autoharp, banjo, keyboard, piano, rhythm machine, etc.

Rhythm instruments: homemade or store-bought.

Back-up music like a karaoke tape or a CD of instrumental music students can sing along with.

List of traditional melodies onto which you can piggyback new words. See page 40 for a partial list of melodies you can use as starting points when composing your songs. Keep adding to the list.

MATERIALS USEFUL FOR THE MUSICAL CLASSROOM

Lyric sheets: For younger students, put all of the favorite classrooms songs on chart paper and have them posted in the music area so that the students can see them at any time. Songs are many children's first link to printed language (most kids sing before they read, at least from my experience). For older students, print lyric sheets of favorite songs, songs that have been written in class, songs written by students individually, class songs, school songs, etc.

Props you may need: Depending on the songs you have written, you may want to design and build scenery, make puppets, cardboard instruments, a little stage area, and any other additional materials that may add to the song.

Easel, marker, pens and/or pencils, tablet of paper (big), or overhead.

Sound system or karaoke machine with mics to use when sharing songs.

Books: Reading books, poetry books, books of movement activities and dance steps to add to the production of classroom songs.

This is my list and it constantly grows. So will yours.

A BIBLIOGRAPHY OF SUGGESTED READING TO STIMULATE SONGWRITING IN THE CLASSROOM

Boyd, Jenny with Holly George-Warren. *Musicians in Tune: Seventy-Five Contemporary Musicians Discuss the Creative Process.* New York: Simon & Schuster, 1992.

Chenfeld, Mimi Brodsky. *Teaching Language Arts Creatively.* 2nd ed. San Diego: Harcourt, 1987.

Copland, Aaron. *Music and Imagination.* Cambridge, MA: Harvard University Press, 1952.

Cox, Terry. *You Can Write Song Lyrics.* Cincinnati: Writer's Digest Books, 2000.

Davis, Sheila. *The Craft of Lyric Writing.* Cincinnati: Writer's Digest Books, 1985.

Gillette, Steve. *Songwriting and the Creative Process.* Bethlehem, PA: Sing Out!, 1995.

Hirschhorn, Joel. *The Complete Idiot's Guide to Songwriting.* Indianapolis: Alpha, 2001.

Hughes, Langston. *The Book of Rhythms.* New York: Oxford USA, 1995.

Lain, Sheryl. *A Poem for Every Student: Creating Community In A Public School Classroom.* Berkeley: National Writing Project, 1998.

Lieberman, Julie Lyonn. *You are Your Instrument: The Definitiv Musician's Guide to Practice and Performance.* New York: Huiksi Music Company, 1991.

Sloan, Carolyn. *Finding Your Voice: A Practical and Spiritual Approach to Singing and Living.* New York: Hyperion, 1999.

Strunk, Jr., William, and E.B. White. *The Elements of Style.* 3rd ed. Boston: Allyn and Bacon, 1979.

Winslow, Robert W. and Dallin, Leon. *Music Skills for Classroom Teachers.* Debuque: Wm. C. Brown Publishers, 1984.

Young, Sue. *The Scholastic Rhyming Dictionary.* New York: Scholastic, 1994.

CHAPTER FIVE

The Songwriting Process

My experiences as a classroom educator and child protection consultant have given me unique insight into the importance of hearing what kids have to say about their lives, the issues they face, the music they listen to, the TV shows they watch, their friends, their families, etc.

After years of working with children, I know they always have a lot on their minds, and that they are very willing to share if given the chance.

And even though most students have many ideas and thoughts to share, I have found some children feel their thoughts are not very important or very creative. To which I always say, "They are to me!" And I mean it. I really care what children have to say, and sometimes conversation just doesn't do justice to their thoughts. Some students have trouble expressing themselves in group discussion situations, and are embarrassed to share their thoughts out loud. I always felt that there had to be a fun, creative, non-threatening way for students to express themselves. I found it in songwriting.

Songwriting is great because anyone can do it, and you can write a song about anything you want. Plus, songwriting can be a group or individual project. Not only can students write about their everyday lives, they can also research and write about topics covered in school lessons or books. In fact, students often write about things that have much importance in their lives like sports, families, friends, environmental concerns, growing up, and of course school. Songwriting stimulates the students' creativity and gets their imaginations going full throttle. Before they know it, the students have enough material for several songs (a key to becoming a good writer is writing, writing and more writing!).

What is a classroom songwriting session like? Is it chaotic, noisy, and out-of-control? No. Songwriting includes several components: active listening, expressing, creating, and sharing. There is so much thinking and brainstorming going on in the classroom that you can almost feel the creative energy. Students wait their turn to share their thoughts as they listen to their classmates' ideas. The excitement builds. The students congratulate each other when a line becomes complete. They constructively question each other when a word or phrase doesn't seem to fit, or is hard to sing. It is a group project from start to finish. With their song nearing completion, congratulations are once again passed around the room and individual critiques of the song are shared. Smiles dominate the faces of every student. (See my notes in Chapter Three regarding feedback. As a teacher, it's your job to moderate the discussion and to make sure that everyone's opinion counts.)

Remember, classroom songwriting has many benefits:

- ✓ It's a fun way to learn.
- ✓ It's a great way for students to hone their research and question-forming skills.
- ✓ It promotes reading (in order to be a good writer/songwriter you need to be a reader).
- ✓ It's a way to help students connect with their own personal creativity and become actively engaged in their own learning process.
- ✓ It's a great way to bring the class together (such as through a group project, like writing a class song).
- ✓ It's a self-esteem builder (sharing ideas takes courage).
- ✓ It helps develop writing skills (having fun plus being creative equals more writing).

Here is the basic outline of my songwriting process. It can be customized for just about any situation, and I'll give some hints on how to use it for some specific purposes later.

Working with Melodies: Many people think that they can't write songs because they don't write music, and they are unsure of how to construct a melody. That's OK, because just about everyone knows hundreds of melodies that they can use as a starting point. Borrowing a known melody has many advantages, especially for younger students.

When you and your class choose the melody in advance, you end up with a pattern that will allow to you to almost automatically fill in the words as you work through the song. The comfort of the known melody will make it easier for your students to focus on the content of the lyrics. The rhythm of the tune will help them edit and put in punctuation.

Piggybacking new words to old tunes is also good training ground for composing new melodies. The more your classroom community works with melodies that you know, the more you will develop a feel for how words can fit with music.

Working with your class, pick a melody that you know and that conveys the feeling that you think your topic is trying to get across. Sometimes, folks actually ask me, "How will I know if I really know the song well enough to use it as a model?" Well, if you can hum it all the way through, with at least fair pitch, and can fit the words with the melody, then you know it. If not, just a little practice won't hurt. You may even want to tape yourself singing the song, and use that as your model if keeping time and tune AND coming up with new words feels like too much brainwork. Just don't let any fears you may have about constructing new melodies prevent you from attempting to write songs.

Here's a list (not at all complete) of common tunes that I always carry with me when I am writing. Please feel free to add to this list. There are enough songs/tunes that you should be able to find one for any set of words that you and your students want to come up with.

Traditional Folk Tunes and Other Songs to Use with Words You Make Up

- A-Hunting We Will Go
- Battle Hymn of the Republic
- Bingo
- Brother John
- Buffalo Gals
- Camptown Races
- Crawdad Song
- Deck the Halls
- Down by the Bay
- Down by the Station
- Duke of York
- Froggie Went A-Courtin'
- Frosty the Snowman
- Go Tell Aunt Rhody
- Goodnight, Irene
- He's got the Whole World in His Hands
- Hole in My Bucket
- Home on the Range
- Home, Sweet, Home
- Hush, Little Baby
- I Dream of Jeanie
- I've Been Workin' on the Railroad
- If You're Happy and You Know It
- John Henry
- Kookabura
- Little Teapot
- Lolly Too-dum
- London Bridge
- Looby Loo
- My Darling Clementine
- Old Lady Who Swallowed a Fly
- Old MacDonald
- Ole Dan Tucker
- Polly-Wolly Doodle
- Pop! Goes the Weasel
- Red River Valley
- Redwing
- Row, Row, Row Your Boat
- She'll Be Comin' Round the Mountain
- Shortnin' Bread
- Skip to My Lou
- Sweet Betsy of Pike
- The Bear Went Over the Mountain
- The Bus Song
- The Hokey Pokey
- The Mulberry Bush

- This Little Light of Mine
- This Old Man
- Three Blind Mice
- Turkey in the Straw
- Twinkle, Twinkle Little Star
- Wayfaring Stranger
- Will the Circle be Unbroken?
- Worried Man Blues
- Yankee Doodle
- Yellow Rose of Texas
- You Are My Sunshine

Select a Topic: When working with a classroom group, brainstorm a list of topics, and list them on the board. Have students vote on their favorite. If students are having trouble picking a topic ask them questions to get them thinking. It is good to have a topic that is interesting to the entire group, and there are many ways to choose song topics. Several topics can be chosen if the class is divided into smaller groups.

The following ideas mostly come from *The Craft of Lyric Writing* by Sheila Davis. These are shortened versions of her ideas with re-writes by me. I wholeheartedly recommend this book for people who really want to get into songwriting. I have added some info myself and have tried to summarize her longer examples for each category.

- ✓ *Local or national newspapers*: Encourage your students to write about current trends, fads, disasters, events, issues. Have them look for humorous headlines and articles that have a human interest.

- ✓ *Favorite magazines and journals*: Again, your students should pick out topics that are interesting to them and their peers.

- ✓ *Current events*: A state's bicentennial, AIDS, elections/politics, diets for the 1990s, the space program, the computer/electronic age, big celebrations (national, state or local), etc.

- ✓ *Popular culture*: Your students could write about their favorite bands, TV shows, movies, clothing styles, foods, etc.

- ✓ **Books**: Your students can make a song out of a favorite line or passage in a book. Books are one of the best places to find lyrics.

- ✓ **Real People**: Encourage your students to write about their parents, a famous person they know or met, a person who has influenced them in sports, music, school work, a friend, a sibling, a singer, an actress, sports hero, the president, etc.

- ✓ **Life**: Tell your students to write about an important event in their life. They should write about things that are important or have meaning to them. Tell them to use their own thoughts, attitudes, and beliefs. Be CREATIVE!!!! Have your students write about doing something that they have never or may never do (e.g. walk on the moon, have lunch with an alien, etc.).

- ✓ **Imagination and dreams**: Often the artistic imagination is a blend of experience and imagination. The imagination takes flight with real events and people, which makes a very interesting song.

- ✓ **Museums/State Archives/Town Records/Older People in Town**: The past is always a great source for lyrics and songs. There are many things from the past worth writing about, e.g. how schools were in the past, a big fire that destroyed part of your town, natural disasters, etc. I have taken groups of students to nursing homes to interview people and we wrote songs from those interviews. Students really enjoyed hearing about the history of their school and the towns they lived in. After writing, rehearsing and recording, we went back to the nursing home and shared our "new" songs. Again, be creative and the sky is the limit.

These are just a few suggestions for teachers and students on topics/themes they might like to write about. Keep in mind that song lyric ideas can come from curriculum/school themes as well.

After picking the topic(s), students may need to do some research before they begin writing. Encourage your students to make up questions that allow the group to explore what they know about the topic already, and what they may need to know or learn in order to make up a song (this is especially true in writing factual or historical stories). Answer all questions that you can on paper, and keep notes for future use.

Brainstorm on the Topic: Once you have picked the topic, you should brainstorm a classroom list of everything that you already know about it, and discuss the results of any research your students have done. List all ideas and known facts as your students say them. Depending on the topic and the type of information discussed, you may want to create categories such as who, what, when, and where, and to group all ideas that are related or could possibly go together. Encourage students to be involved in this process and let everyone know their ideas are important. This is where any questions students weren't able to answer can be discussed. As students share their information and ideas, they can begin to talk about the type of song that they want to create: factual or fictional, experiential, what style of music, type of emotional impact, etc. These ideas of what students are looking for regarding their song will help in the actual writing/composing stages. If you're piggybacking your words to an existing melody, you can help steer the discussion to choosing a song to use as a model.

At this point many writers like to pick a title, and writing a headline or title at top of the paper (or on the board) can help your writers stay focused on the topic. However, you should be prepared to change your chosen title if a better one presents itself later in the writing process.

Come Up with an Opening Line: If you're piggybacking new words to an old tune, begin this step by finalizing your choice of a melody. But as with the title, you should be prepared to change your melody if a better option should present itself. Changing the melody may not be as drastic as it sounds, because many times a given set of words can be sung to different melodies with very little change to the structure of the lines.

Brainstorm opening lines and list them on the board. Say them as a group. Students can use words or lines from their brainstorm lists to form an opening line. Try to sing them. Find an opening line that will lead to a second line. Make sure the line is strong and will be a good lead-in to the rest of the song. Keep the opening lines that aren't used, as you may be able to be use them in one form or another later in the song, or for a second verse. (Remember: **never erase!** Cross out unused lines and ideas so you know what you've tried and what didn't work.)

If your students are having trouble coming up with opening lines, have some or all of them look up and discuss opening lines from their favorite books, poems, or songs. This will generate many ideas and will demonstrate how first lines should lead to second lines, and so on.

Once the opening line is picked, repeat it back again, out loud as a group. Try singing it. Does it flow? Is it too wordy? Don't worry about revision and re-writing here—mostly go for content. You can always come back to edit and reshape. Here you may want to talk about and decide whether or not you'll rhyme it, have a chorus, etc.

Continue to Work on Lines and Verses: Build a second line off the first, keeping in mind the story or idea you are trying get across. Have students use their brainstorming list to form second and third lines. (Encourage your students to go back to their brainstormed lists whenever they get stuck.) After each line is formed, see if it flows and matches the rhythm of the preceding line. Writers sometimes find that a song is made stronger by changing the order of the words, lines, or verses, so you may want to ask if the second line would make a better first line, etc., and you should keep doing this as an exercise as more lines and verses are added.

Focus on generating more lines, and grouping them into verses as the discussion continues. A good way to determine the best order and flow of the lines and verses is by reading them out loud, listening to someone else read them, singing them, or listening to a tape playback of a reading or singing of the song in progress. Listen for ideas and phrases that go together, and for the rhythm and feel of the groupings. Encourage everyone to be involved in the discussion.

Develop the Melody: If you are composing your own melody, discuss the style of the song (country, jazz, folk, ballad, rock n' roll, rap, etc.), and then ask students to look over the first two verses (or as many as are completed) and sing the words and tune the way that they hear them. I believe all words have rhythm and their own musical sounds, and by paying attention to the words and repeating them over and over out loud, the melody and style of the song will evolve almost on its own.

If you are piggybacking new words on an old melody, at this point you may want to ask questions like "Do our words fit the feel of the tune?" You may also want to try your words with a different melody, just to see how a different tune affects the words you've been using.

Revisions, Rewrites, More Drafts: Go over the song line by line. Does it make sense? Does one line lead to the next? Are there any weak lines? Are any lines too wordy or hard to sing? Does the order of any verses need to be changed? Do you understand and comprehend what is being sung? Can words that are overused or lacking in energy be replaced by more active, exciting, emotional words? Does the song have a steady rhythm that flows from start to finish? Do the words do justice to the title? Changes in the melody, chorus, bridge, style, emotion, etc., can be done during this stage of the writing. Remember most of us aren't just writers, we are re-writers.

Add Instrumental or Rhythmic Accompaniment: Guitars, banjos, recorders, autoharps, rhythm instruments, homemade instruments, hand claps, knee slaps, toe taps, and thigh whaps can all be used for accompaniment. To me the most important thing to keep in mind here is to get a beat going—the rhythm brings the words and song alive. It gives breath to the words and brings life to the song. A metronome, drum machine or click track of an electric keyboard can also be used. If no accompaniment is available, sing it *a cappella* with feeling. Again, remember that the beat is so important. If you are not musically inclined, have the music teacher (or a volunteer parent) accompany the class and further develop the song. During this stage movement and drama can be added to the song and will add to the rhythm. (Movements can be sign language, full-body gestures, dance, and drama, including tableau, mirroring, and acting out each line.)

Reshaping/Fine-tuning/Polishing of Drafts and Revisions: This is basically pulling together the song and adding finishing touches. The floor should be open for a final brainstorming session where the student writers can share their thoughts and offer ideas on any last minute/final changes. During this stage the ending will probably be re-written many times as the students work on it and sing it several times. The goal is to keep the discussion active, and to make sure everyone contributes their ideas.

Record the Song and Add It to Your Classroom List of Songs to Sing: The song does not have to be complete in order to record it and play it back. Active listening is a very big part of songwriting, and many times, after listening to playbacks, students do more fine tuning or adding of verses. Good listening skills are so important in songwriting.

Share Your Song: Sing it as a whole group and record it. Make tapes that students can take home and share with their friends, siblings, parents, grandparents, etc. Sing the song to other classes, play the recording (or sing it live) during morning announcements or before an all-school assembly. Send a copy of the song (on audio or video tape), with lyric sheet, to students in the same grade at another school in another town or state. Ask them to listen and to list all information that they learned from the song. Ask your school music teacher for advice on expanding the song (e.g., adding instruments, rhythm, drama, or movement). Have them help you compose and write out your own melody with harmonies. Music teachers will have many ideas—don't forget to work with them during your songwriting process.

CUSTOMIZING THE SONGWRITING PROCESS

This basic songwriting process can be customized for just about any purpose. I've used it with young kids, old kids, teachers, business people, and with everyone in between. Just about anyone—even those that don't think they can be writers—can compose using my songwriting process.

I have used my songwriting process with kids of all ages. Here is an example of how I use it with kindergarten and early first-grade songwriters.

Songwriting with kids this young is highly successful, works well with emergent reading, and goes with my philosophy that writing activities and "finished products" can always grow with a writer's knowledge of writing craft and language. The children generally "get it," it's easy to expand, and it convincingly demonstrates how young writers can get better with practice. Encouraging young, emergent writers to keep a portfolio of their work is a great way to show them where they started, where they have been, and where they can go.

Get all your students involved, try to generate some excited discussion, and pick a topic. Ask questions to keep the discussion moving. Listen to everyone's ideas.

Once you have picked the topic, you can write it on the board or at the top of a piece of chart paper—having a headline to describe the topic definitely helps keep young writers focused on what they are writing about. Some kids might already have a title in mind—picking the title at this point is okay, but remember to be willing to let it go if it takes away from the creative process or causes writers to get hung up.

Have your young writers brainstorm and give you four lines or ideas (kindergarten) or eight lines or ideas which you will encourage them to develop into at least 16 (first and second graders) as the songwriting process moves on. Depending on age and developmental level, you may get one word, two or three words, or actual sentences. My experience is that the more the children have been read to and have experienced books on their own, the better they are with the writing process and the more words they give me. (What better way for kids to experience language at its best than by exposing them to books? The benefits are many and will extend into all areas of a student's life.) If the group appears stuck, I will offer hints and suggestions, more likely than not in question form, to help them obtain the information they need to write about the topic they have chosen.

Have the group pick a common tune that all the students know forwards and backwards to write their song to. Especially with younger students, using a known melody allows them to focus on the content of the song. The familiarity of the rhythm and melody can be comforting and allows them to generate more ideas.

So, if kindergarteners choose the topic "Pets" and give me as their brainstorm list of words (or lines) "Dogs," "Kitties," "Birds," and "Ponies," I would take a song like "Jingle Bells" and sing the four words they gave me about pets:

Dogs
Kitties
Birds
Ponies

I sing the words first to the verse and then to the chorus, just repeating the same word over and over again. I point out how singing what we've just written to the tune we've picked lets us know that we need more words. So I start combining their words into lines and I sing them again:

Dogs and kitties,
Birds and ponies.

I show them that adding a few words makes the lines easier to sing and to read. I continue to ask them questions about what have we written so far. Does it make sense? Is it teaching or telling us anything? What can we learn from the words so far?

Then I start asking them questions about what each animal does. I write their new brainstorming down and add it to the lines. After everyone has had the chance to share their ideas, we may end up with something like this:

Dogs like to bark.
Kitties like to play,
Birds like to fly,
Ponies like to run.

On the last line some kids may say, "Ponies like to ride." So I ask them, do ponies ride ponies? Who rides ponies? I may ask, what do ponies do best? Or, what do they do when they are around other ponies? Here you may get "eat," "fight," and "run." Discuss your options, and again, try to get everyone to contribute.

At this point it is a good idea to number the lines of the song, so you can refer to them easily and experiment with the order that they come in. Discuss the different options with your students. Have them vote on which order and combinations work best.

With kindergarteners, you may stop with these words the first time through and **ask the kids to give you movement ideas,** or maybe show them how to do the song in sign language. Turn your song into a circle dance. Do it call and response. Sing it to "Skip to My Lou" or "A-Hunting We Will Go" or any other song your students know and love. (Trying your words with different melodies can help your students revise any lines that may not make sense, or that need tweaking.)

With first-graders, I like to **spread re-writes over a period of time.** I encourage them to make up a line to answer each existing line so that we can double the length of our first verse. Then I work with them to either develop a new idea into a second verse, or to choose an idea from the first verse that can be used to move the song into a second verse.

Through repetition, I can see how well they are reading, writing, singing, and understanding. They tell me when to move on. (As the Buddhist maxim says, "When the student is ready, the teacher appears.") You should **keep coming back to the song** every few days or every couple of weeks and see what words can be added as your students' language and vocabulary skills grow. Look at each line and see if anything could be added or taken away, or if some of the lines could be developed into new verses, or if the order of the verses can be adjusted. Turn the song into a story, or a book, or a skit, or a dance.

After spending time with the song, and after several revisions, it may end up looking something like this:

Dogs like to bark
When they see people
Kitties like to play
With other kitties.
Birds like to fly

Up in the sky.
Ponies like to run
Very fast.

If you want your students to end up with a more personalized song, then you can vary the questions that you ask while generating discussion. Using "who," "what," "where," "when," "why" and "how," and asking them for their personal opinions based on what they think, what they know, what they have read, what they have heard, and what they have experienced will yield a personal song. For example:

I like dogs
Dogs bark loud.
I like kitties
Kitties like to play.
I like birds
Birds fly high.
I like ponies
I wish I could ride.

Depending on what you ask during your brainstorming sessions, your song can go in many different directions. Of course, that is what creativity is all about. I want students to connect with the writing process, and to learn that they are indeed writers and meaning makers. Using my songwriting process is a great way to get them started.

Even if you only have a few minutes to devote to the process, songwriting is an effective teaching tool. I have generated songs that students love to sing in as little as 45 minutes. Just remember to keep the discussion moving, give everyone the opportunity to participate, and listen to everyone's suggestions.

A FEW CLOSING THOUGHTS ON SONGWRITING

Remind your students that to be good writers they must also be good readers. Reading stories, poems, historical pieces, and other literature feeds the imagination and provides great ideas for opening lines, titles, and songs. I use good writing as a model and as inspiration for my own writing. Reading and writing go together just like students and teachers!

Of course, the real key to successful writing is to write and write and then write some more. You'll only get better with experience.

Students often ask me about where good lyrics come from. Well, I find ideas that can lead to good lyrics everywhere! I mean that. In the past 25 years I have found ideas for songs at airports, schools, sports events, shopping malls, on school buses, at meetings, nursing homes, child care centers, and schools: Basically, everywhere and anywhere that there are people using real language to communicate with each other.

I am also often asked how I know that a song idea will be successful. I quickly point out that as a writer I do not always know where an idea will lead me or whether or not that idea, in its present form, will become a song. To me, discovering where the songwriting journey takes me is more than half the fun of writing.

In fact, let students know that finished products are great and something to be proud of, but that the writing process is the big event. If students can learn to love the writing process they will discover much about themselves, how they learn, and how to be creative. When a writer is process-based as opposed to end-product-based, there is no failure.

It's good for writers (especially for beginning writers) to be realistic and write about things that they have interest in, and to write from the heart. Passion is a wonderful thing for writers to have. Having passion and the ability to love the writing process can only help your great ideas become great songs.

Great song lyrics are often based on ideas that everyone can relate to and understand in their own personal way. It could be a song about school, a favorite teacher, a great book, a funny personal experience, friends, family, and other "real" experiences that each of us will encounter at some time in our lives (for example, there are certain rituals and age-related events that we all eventually go through—these can make great songs if written well).

There is not much that is more rewarding than to have people (friends or total strangers) nod their heads as you sing your song, keeping time with the rhythm and flow, and then to have them say to you, "Man, I have felt that same way so many times" or "Gee, I know just what you are talking about" or, as one of my students said to me, "You know, Gary, I could have written that song myself." When you get listeners and readers to respond like this you have found success as a writer. To me, nothing else matters.

When I write, I follow a few simple guidelines: I write my worst first, I always write to a rhythm or beat to get a flow or pattern going, I write from the heart to keep the human element in my songs, and I try to have a purpose or message even if the purpose or message is to get people to laugh and have fun.

So what else makes a good song? A title that everyone will remember. A good title captures the listener's interest and invites them to listen to the words. I always keep a section in my writing notebook for titles that I make up or overhear (usually the person saying the phrase that I am guessing will make a great title has no idea that they are saying something I like). These possible titles may or may not inspire me to write any lyrics in the future, but it is always good to have choices to work with. My list of possible titles just keeps growing and growing every day.

Songwriting is good for putting closure on events in your life. Suggest that your students write a song if they seem upset about the end of school year, or a classmate moving away, etc. Songwriting can help them work out the feelings and emotions of the experience, then turn the page and move on.

Songwriting can also be a way of reviewing what you've done, or memorializing events like field trips or special visits. Encourage your students to answer questions like, "What did you learn from the experience? How will the experience influence your life in coming years? What did the experience teach you about yourself? About other people?"

Remember, one song leads to another, and before you know it you have a classroom of eager, creative writers ready to write. Learning should be fun, and kids really have fun working their ideas into songs.

CHAPTER SIX

My Teacher Rides a Harley: There's a Song for Everything and Every Day

Being a songwriter and musician has made it easy for me to find music to use for teaching all parts of the curriculum. I have been collecting songs for years: I get them from folk archives, modern recordings, and musicians I meet on the street. In my travels I continue to meet teachers throughout the United States who know that music is a great teaching tool for all subjects, especially reading.

These songs appear on the CD that's included with this book. I encourage you to use them in your classroom, for sing-alongs and the activities they inspire.

1. Read Songs Sing Books
2. Pages from the Past
3. Macaroni & Cheese
4. The Homework Blues
5. Leroy the Kitty
6. Different, Yet the Same
7. I'm a Razzle-Dazzle Reader
8. We like Frogs

9. If You Sit by Me
10. The New Three Little Pigs
11. My Teacher Rides a Harley
12. Mazi, My Boy
13. Mummies Made in Egypt
14. My Teacher Thinks He's Elvis
15. I Want a Good Book to Read
16. Read Songs Sing Books (Reprise)

When I'm introducing a song to students, I usually teach it to them call and response (a style of singing where a chorus of singers responds to or echoes a lead singer). I'll sing the line first, teaching the kids the words and introducing them to the melody, and then they sing it back to me.

Especially if you aren't using instruments like guitar or keyboards to accompany you when singing these songs, simple rhythm instruments such as rhythm sticks, handle castanets, jingle sticks, or hardwood sand blocks can add an extra dimension. Remember that hand claps, thigh whaps, and finger snaps are great for keeping rhythm and adding some accompaniment.

After each song, I have included a list of follow-up activities and ideas that I like to use to encourage kids to be creative and express their feelings and knowledge in new ways. These activities have been tried and tested across the U.S. and will help bring more music and creativity into your daily teaching. However, these activities are just a start. I encourage all teachers who read this book to make up their own.

READ SONGS SING BOOKS

This song was written during a teacher workshop. I basically wanted to sum up what reading is all about, and to explore the close connection that songs and books have.

I go to the library or a bookstore
I find a good book I want to explore.
I get myself cozy. I sit on the floor.
I read, read, read. Then I read some more.

After some reading, I try something new,
Just a little literary switcheroo.
(I) start with one page, then I try two,
(I) build a little rhythm – a little zip-pi-dee-doo.

('Cause) I like to read and I like to sing.
I like a good book with words that ring.
With words that rock and words that swing
I want a good book that I can sing.

MUSICAL EXTENSIONS AND ACTIVITIES

- Have your students write songs about the pleasures they get from reading. Introduce the activity with a class discussion on the similarities between songs and books.

- This song belongs to the same family as "I'm A Razzle-Dazzle Reader" (page 82) and "I Want a Good Book to Read" (page 109). Some of the follow-up activities for those songs can be used with this song as well.

I wrote this song with Brod Bagert (a wonderful writer and children's performance poet) as a celebration of great literature.

> White gave us a spider
> And Charlotte was her name,
> And she taught a pig named Wilbur
> That life was not a game.
>
> And life out on the prairie is
> What Laura Ingalls knew,
> The children in her books
> Are just like me and you.
>
> *It's like a play inside me*
> *And I make up the cast,*
> *I travel far and wide with them*
> *On pages from the past.*
>
> And Edgar Allen Poe
> Wrote stories dark and grim,
> I like to read his stories
> But I'm kind of scared of him.
>
> And Alcott's little women
> And Mark Twain's boy named Finn
> In books I never lose a friend
> In books I always win.
>
> *Chorus*

MUSICAL EXTENSIONS AND ACTIVITIES

- This song is a model for a cool project you can do in your classroom. Introduce it early in the school year, and then each time you finish reading a book, have your students write a two- to four-line summary identifying its main ideas, and then add verses to the song. This would be a great year-long project.

- Another project would be to set a history of children's literature to music. Have your students research what books and authors were popular with kids during particular periods of time. Then, using "Pages from the Past" as a model, have them develop a song. The song could cover book titles, authors' names, how children's books have changed, etc. This would be a great way to learn about children's literature.

- Have your students write a song honoring all of the great writers from your state or town. Give them time to research the authors first, and then lead them through the process of turning what they know into verses for the song. Again, this is a great way to see how much they know about the authors. Below is a sample I wrote for the Montana State Reading Association. Hopefully it will give you a few ideas on a project for your state or area.

- Remember, once a song is written, that doesn't mean you're done with it. A song like this can be re-written, updated, and expanded all the time. Have your students make illustrations to go with the words, and then put them into book form.

- A fine resource for this writing project is Scholastic's *The Author Studies Handbook: Helping Students Build Powerful Connections to Literature* by Laura Kotch and Leslie Zackman.

MONTANA READERS

There are leaders
Who are readers
In the state of Montana.
From Wibaux to Troy
And all towns in between.
They're spreading the joy
To every girl and boy.
The joy of being a reader
In the Big Sky Country.

Come join the readers.
Come join the leaders.
Come read with me...
In the Big Sky Country.

Burning like a wild fire
Is *Rescue Josh McGuire.*
The love for this book
Is blazing out of control.
Thanks to Ben and Buffy
This story came to be
About a boy and a bear
Surviving in the Big Sky Country.

Chorus

There are books like *Killing Custer*
Tell the fate of the Plains Indians.

And books like *Winter Wheat*
'Bout a young woman's journey.
There are books of every topic
Montana has to offer
Including *The Big Sky*
By A. B. Guthrie.

Chorus

(Can be sung to "Ghost Riders In The Sky")

MACARONI & CHEESE

So many kids love macaroni and cheese that I just felt there had
to be a song about it. I added the part about Elvis because I read
that he loved macaroni and cheese, too.

Macaroni and ch-ch-ch-cheese (3xs)
Macaroni and cheese!

It is my favorite food,
Macaroni and cheese.
I eat it every day
Whenever I please.
To me it's even better
Than bagels and lox
And when I'm with my grandpa
He lets me eat the whole box....of

Chorus

They serve it at my school.
They serve it in Paris, France.
They serve it in fancy restaurants
Where grownups kiss and dance.
When Mom bakes it in the oven
It really melts the cheese.
Which grosses (for younger kids: scares) out my
brother
'Cause it looks like someone sneezed....on his

Chorus

Sometimes my older sister
Really likes to tease
Saying that she ate
All the macaroni and cheese.

But I get the last laugh
As she opens up my closet door.
She's conked on the head
And knocked to the floor...by 31,693 hidden boxes of

Chorus

Homemade, thick and gooey,
Always sure to please.
Baked or boiled.
Made with A-merican a-cheese.
I can eat it at the table
Or sitting on my knees.
Elvis even loved it
Macaroni and cheese, uh-huh, uh-huh, uh-huh.

Chorus

(Then, using the 5 main long vowels, sing it like this)

Macarana ane chaise
Meekeereenee eene cheese
Micirini ine chise
Mocorono oan chose
Mucurunu une choose

Chorus

 MUSICAL EXTENSIONS AND ACTIVITIES

- This is a fun song for me to sing because it has a nice melody
  and I never quite sing it the same way twice. I sing the chorus
  in a call and response fashion, with me singing the "macaroni"
  and the kids singing the "ch-ch-cheese."

- Add rhythm to the song to help accentuate the beats on the "ch-ch-cheese" parts. This song sounds great with tasteful percussion.

- Have a macaroni and cheese party in your class and have the students make up new verses to the song based on their experiences eating macaroni and cheese during the classroom party (or at home or in a restaurant).

- This song shows that you can write about any subject and have people enjoy it. Students tell me it makes them hungry. After hearing it, many people have related their funny experiences with macaroni and cheese.

- Have your students write a song about items that don't seem like obvious song subjects. As always, have the students share their creations. Fun projects like this give students a creative break when they have been working hard, and can get the creative juices going for the next classroom project.

THE HOMEWORK BLUES

The idea for this song first came up during an after-school detention session that the principal just happened to drag me along to. (The kids were sure that I had detention either because of my long hair or because of the way I acted. Good guesses on both accounts.) We came up with an incredible list of excuses on why we couldn't do our homework. As we ran them by the principal he either yawned or shook his head. They finally figured out that it actually took less time to do your homework than to try to come up with excuses that work. From that came "The Homework Blues."

Health homework's due,
Lesson number nine.
Teacher asks me if it's done,
I feed her a line...
Did she believe me?
Did she believe me?
Now I'm in the office doin' my time.

(In) good old Math
Lesson number two
My homework's not done
What am I gonna do?
I'll have to stay.
I'll have to stay.
(I'll) have to stay after school
And you know that isn't cool.

First it was Health.
Then it was Math.
Why can't you follow
That homework path?
What's your excuse?

65

What's your excuse?
I think that you've got the homework blues.

First it was Health.
Then it was Math.
Now I'm a-followin'
That homework path.
No excuses.
No excuses.
Teacher, I no longer have
The homework blues.

 ## MUSICAL EXTENSIONS AND ACTIVITIES

- This song is best sung call and response, with the last line of
  each verse sung in unison.

- Make a classroom chart of every excuse your students have
  given (or that they can think of) as to why they didn't get
  their homework done.

- Have your students question their parents, grandparents,
  siblings, friends, and neighbors on the best excuses they have
  ever used for not doing their homework. Compare those
  excuses with your own class list. Same or different?

- Have students write a story (fictional or non-fictional) on the
  most outrageous excuse they have used for not doing their
  homework. Encourage students to act out their stories using
  sound effects, funny faces, etc. Tell them to be dramatic. Great
  stories can be turned into a play and shared with other classes.

- Ask your students to write a pretend letter to their teacher,
  their parents, the president of the U.S., the principal, etc.,
  explaining why they just couldn't do their homework last night.

- Make up another list to hang up in the classroom on all of the benefits of studying, doing homework, going to school, putting your heart into your work, etc. Have your students write a song based on the list.

- Have students research when, where, and why schools were first started in the U.S., their home state, or their hometown. Encourage them to find out why their school was originally started, why it is named what it is named, etc. Ask your students to look for any information on when and why homework came to be.

- To expand this activity, have students interview their relatives, their neighbors, their parents, their grandparents, etc., on what kinds of and how much homework they had when they were in school. Share with classmates what you found out, including samples of old homework (I have some amazing assignments from the 1930s and 40s). Have students share what they learned regarding the history of homework and any old samples they found. Lead a discussion of how homework today compares with homework in the past. Is school harder now than it was then? Is it even possible to make a comparison betweens schools of yesterday and today? Why or why not?

LEROY THE KITTY

This song was written for Leroy, my mom and dad's cat. He was a cool, music-loving kitty. I believe Leroy would have loved going to school with my younger brother Mark. For a cat he had a fairly good attention span (much longer than mine) and he always seemed to listen to us when we discussed things at my parent's home. I was always waiting for him to jump in on the conversations, but he never did. Rest in Peace, Leroy.

Leroy was a kitty
Who couldn't go to school
He had no kitty books
To learn the kitty rules
He stayed upon the farm
Which did him no harm
But what he really wanted
Was to go to school.

So one day the teacher
Was walking down the lane
She saw Little Leroy
Sittin' in the rain
She said Little Leroy
Would you like to come to school
So she gave him some kitty books
To learn the kitty rules.

Now Leroy is so happy
As he walks on to school
Singing the kitty songs
That all good kitties do
Readin', writin', 'rithmetic,
Mousing as well
Leroy likes his school
As his teacher rings the bell.

- This song is best sung as a group, with everybody singing together.

- Lead the children in making up more verses about Leroy, about Leroy wanting to go to school, why he couldn't go to school, etc.

- Have your students write about their own pets in school. Their stories, poems, or songs could include how their pet got to school, what subjects their pet studied, what their pet ate for lunch, what their pet did on recess, and what their pet's school day would be like. This can be done as a whole-class, small-group, or individual activity.

- Make up a school book for Leroy the Kitty that has his kitty songs, kitty math, kitty reading, kitty writing, etc. Your students could make up math enrichment problems, spelling exercises, and more for Leroy to do.

- Illustrate each verse and turn the song into a book.

- Begin a research project on cats. Have children discuss different types of cats and where they come from. Make a chart and discuss the differences between tame cats and wild cats such as lions, tigers, cheetahs, bobcats, pumas, leopards, etc.

- Have your students research and collect other songs about cats. Write them out on chart paper. Are there facts to learn from these songs? What are these songs like? Fiction? Non-fiction? Funny?

- Beatrix Potter wrote a wonderful story about Thomas Kitten, a real kitten who has some human-like qualities. It's great to read this story with your students and then to re-write it, add drama, visual arts, and sign language. Compare Thomas to Leroy the Kitty, the kitty who went to school.

- Ask your students to write a song or story about the one thing they would do if they were a cat. Encourage them to be creative and think about all of the things that cats do. This activity will be more successful if you allow some time for your students to do research about cats. A brainstorming session would be very helpful.

- Search for poetry about cats (such as T. S. Eliot's "The Naming of Cats") and poetry using images of cats (Carl Sandburg's "Fog"). After reading and discussing the "cat" poetry, have students write their own poems about cats and cat-like images. They could begin by doing re-writes of the poems they have read.

- A school for kitties might be different from a school for kids. Have students research different types of schools: schools with no walls, music schools, magnet schools, art schools, sports schools, private schools, military schools, schools on military bases, year-round schools, Native American reservation schools, etc. What do these schools have in common? How are they different? Students may want to consider length of the school day, the curriculum, the number of students, the make up of the school's population (ethnic backgrounds), types of buildings/structures, objectives/goals, length of school year, criteria for attending, etc. To extend this project look at schools from around the world. Again focus on similarities and differences between these schools and United States schools. When looking at areas of studies in foreign schools, do research on how they teach foreign languages and how many languages students at these schools can learn. This project is a great lead-in to establishing pen pals from other schools all over the world.

- Your students can become pen pals with children from another school in your town or state, or in other states or countries. When writing letters, your students can ask their pen pals to tell them about their school, the student body, what the school is famous or known for, its mission statement, what areas of study are offered, special events celebrated by the school, etc. Be sure to share pictures, writings, or perhaps even a video about your school. Students could also collect leaves, pine cones, flowers, rocks, or other natural specimens indigenous to your area to send to pen pal school (in return, they can send the same). Meeting and getting to know people from other areas helps break down the barriers and prejudices that we sometimes form about the unknown. After corresponding with pen pals, students often find that they are more similar then they might have thought.

DIFFERENT, YET THE SAME

As I travel to different schools around the country, most of the things that I see are positive, although I do occasionally see things that are downright ugly and wrong—like racism. I have witnessed fights and altercations at schools over differences of opinions as students fail to accept and respect someone for who they are. I wrote this song after one such event left a huge impression on me.

> We were talking in class
> Just the other day
> How we all are different
> Yet, the same in different ways.
>
> It really got us thinking
> As we looked around the class.
> No one was in a hurry,
> But we were glancing mighty fast.
>
> Pencils were drawn,
> Paper in place.
> A thoughtful look
> Was on each face.
> Our list began
> With the basic facts
> How we all are the same,
> Yet, not exact.
>
> Most folks have hair,
> Two eyes and two feet,
> Arms, hands and fingers,
> Two knees and a seat.

A mouth and nose,
And two ears to hear.
But after the basics
The differences appear.

Some have red hair.
Some have brown.
Some wear it short.
Some wear it down.

Some have green eyes
And some have blue.
Some wear glasses
And contacts, too.

All of our bodies
Are covered with skin.
Though different in color,
We are the same within.

We all have a mind
To think and create,
To reason and hear
What others relate.

Though we may not agree
With other points of view,
We learn to listen
And accept them, too.

We all have a voice
To speak from the heart.
We think 'fore we speak,
But we take part.

In conversation or song
Both short and long.
With voice we express
For we all belong.

Our list got longer
As the day wore on.
Different, yet the same,
Became our song. (*repeat*)

MUSICAL EXTENSIONS AND ACTIVITIES

The Same in Different Ways: Writing a School Song

Writing a school song is a great way to bring unity to your student body. When writing a school song, students become aware of how we all are the same, how we are all different, and how who we are adds to the color, life, and excitement of the school. It's a great learning experience for everyone involved.

School songs should have a strong central theme, should tell about the school's history, and should include an exploration of who makes up the school's population. A school song should be positive, offer a message that brings students and staff together, and identify the goals, philosophies and objectives of the school. Most of all, a school song should be composed of sincere, well chosen words. After all, this song will identify and represent the whole school and the surrounding community.

I am not saying a school song will cure all your people-related ills, but it's a start. It gets the communication going, and gives the students ownership of the school-wide community that their input helps define. Any project that you can do that gets students to relax, laugh a little, think critically, actively listen, and express themselves in a safe way can't be all that bad.

I have put together some research questions for your students to answer. By answering all or some of them you will find the information that you need to write your school song. (Some of these research activities are similar to the activities listed for "The Homework Blues" (page 65). Consider working with both projects at the same time. I think kids get excited when they discover that the work they do for one project can also be used for another project.)

Read through these suggestions, and then compile a customized list of questions that relate to your particular school. Give a copy of your questions to the student council, all the classroom teachers, and the administrative staff. List them in the school newspaper and send notes home to parents. Try to get everyone involved in the research process.

You might want to get the larger school community involved as well. List your questions in the town newspaper, and let readers know that you are also looking for general information on the history of the school. Perhaps you could arrange for some alumni, or a town historian, to come answer questions at a school assembly.

Some schools divide the research questions by classroom, so that each class is only responsible for two or three. Answers are sent to a central group that is in charge of compiling the research and writing the song. Included in this group might be music teachers, community reps, other faculty members, and a student representative from each class.

After the song is written, the student representatives take it to their respective classrooms for changes, edits, and general feedback. Often, more than one version of the song emerges, and the student body has to vote on the final draft after hearing both versions performed during the morning announcements.

This activity really can bring a school together. It offers students the opportunity to have an investment in something that is dear to their hearts, helps with school spirit, and can be enjoyed by the community at large. If you're having trouble getting the classroom chemistry to jell, writing a class song can be a great icebreaker.

Again, use these questions as a starting point. Customize your list to highlight the specialized history and peculiarities of your particular school. Remember that by acknowledging our similarities **and** our differences, we can begin to have open discussions and to experience real unity.

- What are your favorite subjects? Who are your favorite teachers? What is your favorite extra-curricular activity? What are the things about your school that you like the best?

- Who makes up the population of your school? The population of the community that supports your school? In what ways (personal, educational, athletic, or cultural) are students at your school the same? Different?

- When was your school founded? By whom? Why was the school started? Is this the original site of the school? The original building? See if you can arrange interviews with town elders who may be former students or retired teachers.

- What are your school's philosophies, goals, and objectives? Have they changed since the school was started? Does your school have an official mission statement?

- How can personal differences affect a school? Are differences respected, accepted, and/or tolerated at your school?

- What purpose does a mascot serve for a school? For the community? What is your school's mascot? What is the history behind how and when your mascot was chosen? Has it ever changed or been revised? Does your mascot have anything to do with your school's stated mission?

- Is there anything special that your school is known for? Has your school always had a reputation for this?

- Is there a unifying force, event, or person that brings your class and/or school together?

- Why is your school (your education, your friends, your teachers) important to you?

- What does being a student at your school mean to you? What are your responsibilities as a student at your school? To yourself? To your teachers? To your classmates and peers?

- How do the similarities and differences in your community add to life in the school?

- Does your school have any regularly occurring projects, events, traditions, or celebrations that help bring the staff, students and greater school community together?

- If someone asked you to describe your school in ten words or less what would you say? Try to come up with a list that covers as many aspects of school life as you can. Describe the school grounds, the atmosphere, the students, the teachers, etc. Keep the diversity of the student body in mind, and make note of special student talents, the subjects offered, the staff and administration, the neighboring community(s), field trips, etc.

- Make a list of words describing your school, your community, your friends, your teachers, your mentors. Make a separate category for each. Are there similarities with each list? Are the words from all lists connected somehow?

- We sometimes do not accept people who are different, or we find it difficult to listen to and accept opinions that are different from our own. How does your school address this problem?

- Respect is an important word. In what ways should you

respect the opinions of your peers and teachers? Do students, teachers, and community members generally accept and respect people for who they are?

- How can we learn from each other's backgrounds and personal experiences? How can learning about each other's lives bring a school together?

- What does your school do that encourages students to be unique individuals, but also team players in cooperative learning experiences?

- What kinds of contributions can students make to their school? In the past year how have the current students improved your school?

- Are all students encouraged to become a part of the greater school community? Do the teachers and students help others who are struggling to fit in? What types of activities are offered by teachers to bring students together?

- What issues and concerns is your school facing? Racism, student violence, apathy? Accepting all people for who they are? How are these issues/concerns positively dealt with? What tools are used to prevent them from reaching crisis levels?

- Do all the students at your school have a voice? Do you feel that you can share your opinions in a safe way even if the teachers or administrators disagree? Does your school have a system for hearing concerns from students and a forum where student concerns can be shared?

- What are your school colors? What do they represent? What do the colors mean to the students and staff?

- How is your school involved with the greater school community? How is the greater school community involved with the school?

- What are you most proud about your school? How do the teachers, administrators, staff, and school board members encourage school pride and school spirit? How are parents involved in school pride and school spirit?

- How do students participate in the running of the school? Do students have a real voice in issues? In rule making? Are students involved in discipline matters for peers?

- Why is getting a good education important to you? Does your school meet your needs educationally? Emotionally? Creatively? Are you challenged every day? Do you contribute as an equal team player with your teachers in making sure that you get the best education that you can? Is there anything you would change (other than getting rid of all teachers, administrators, rules, and homework)? What would you change? How could these changes positively affect and improve your education?

- What is the best thing about the grade level you are in? What are the biggest challenges your grade faces?

Here is an example of a song that was written as a community project to save a neighborhood school that was going to be closed. Since the students were scheduled to be shipped off to other schools (which were already crowded enough), the new schools were not happy about the old school closing either. They told me they needed a unifying song that would bring the school family together along with the folks from the other school communities where these students would be going. So, I did research, and asked tons of questions. I picked a Civil Rights-era tune—"This Little Light of Mine"—to piggyback new words on, so people would just be learning new words and not a new melody. Then, using feedback from parents, students, teachers, and members of the community, we wrote this song. It was used during the campaign to save the school (which is still open).

THIS LITTLE SCHOOL OF MINE
(To the tune of "This Little Light of Mine")

This little school of mine,
We're gonna let it shine.
This little school of mine,
We're gonna let it shine.
This little school of mine,
We're gonna let it shine.
Let it shine! Let it stand! Let it be!

The Gerry (pronounced "Gary") School is a fine school,
We're gonna let it shine.
Built in 19 hundred six,
It still looks mighty fine.
Sits high on a hill in Marblehead,
A historic part of town.
This old school has a lot to give
Let it shine, don't tear it down.

Chorus

Gerry School is a neighborhood school
Where families rally round.
When a project needs to be done,
The parents can be found.
Giving their time and support
The parents will always come through.
They believe in the school with spirit
And hope you'll believe in Gerry, too.

Chorus

80

And Gerry is a learning school,
The teachers give their best.
They all believe in excellence
And the children pass the test.
Old Gerry's weathered the waves of time
And steered her children clear.
Now we must fight for Gerry
And that is why we're here!

Chorus

As 19 hundred 91
Moves along each day.
We know the times are getting rough
And we've all got to change our ways.
But we believe in the school with spirit
And she has to give
Let Gerry stand!
Let Gerry live!

Chorus

I'M A RAZZLE-DAZZLE READER

Reading is an incredible skill that we all need for fun, for work, for survival, and for learning. Reading—like singing and writing—is a celebration of language. It helps everyone gain and develop the skills necessary to creatively and clearly communicate with others. I can't begin to say how important reading is.

Kids don't like it when we teach and preach, but love it when we find a way to stimulate, motivate, and encourage learning in a fun, creative way. That's why I've written so many songs that are fun to sing, but yet promote literacy. "I'm A Razzle-Dazzle Reader" was inspired by my good friend, Daphne Platts, Director of the Sublette County Public Library in Pinedale, Wyoming.

> I'm a razzle-dazzle reader
> I read every day
> All kinds of books
> In all kinds of ways.
> I read standin' up, sittin' down,
> Or lyin' on my bed.
> I read on the school bus
> Or standin' on my head.
> I read fiction, history,
> Poetry and prose.
> I'm a razzle-dazzle reader
> And everyone knows.
>
> Monday to the library
> Right after school.
> Mysteries and adventures—
> These books are cool.
> My brother loves sports books
> To that I can attest.
> An athlete he's not,
> But he can read with the best.

'Cause he's a razzle-dazzle reader
And he reads every day.

I have a little sister—
She likes big picture books,
When she tries to read
Her face has a funny look.
But one of these days
She'll be able to read
Any book or story
That she may please.

'Cause she's a razzle-dazzle reader
And she reads every day.

My friends and I like camping
Taking long hikes,
Paddling a canoe,
And riding our bikes.
But if anyone asks me
What's my favorite thing to do
I pull out my favorite book
I read a page or two.

'Cause I'm a razzle-dazzle reader
And I read every day.

Teacher!!! I don't need free pizza
To make me read.
Teacher!!!! You don't have to eat worms
Just to get me to read.
I read 'cause I want to
No gimmicks need apply
'Cause reading is a skill
I can use my whole life.

So now you must remember
What the book doctors say,
"A good book a day
Keeps illiteracy away."
To read a good story
Is food for the mind
You have to read to write
And that's not a line.

(*Fade out with jazz scat*)

 ## MUSICAL EXTENSIONS AND ACTIVITIES

This song has been used by hundreds of schools, libraries, and reading councils for the slogans of their reading programs. "Razzle-Dazzle Reader" tee-shirts have been made, as well as banners, fliers, and posters. Down in Guatemala City they turned the song into a play.

Have your students write slogans, songs, poems, and stories that celebrate reading, writing, and language in general. Have fun with it. Be creative. A little razzle-dazzle in every classroom never hurt anyone.

One of my favorite projects related to this song is to get all teachers, staff, parents, and students writing songs to promote reading and writing in school. If we are going to encourage the students to read and write, shouldn't we, as adults, be showing them good examples?

The following little ditties to promote reading and writing were all written to the tune of "Row, Row, Row Your Boat." Once they were composed, we put them on banners and posted them throughout the school and the community. It's a great way to get people talking about reading and writing, and it's great fun as well.

LITTLE DITTIES ON READING (hint: when singing the following ditties it's good to sing to a beat. It really helps with the phrasing.)

Read, read, read a book out loud or to yourself, when you're done close your book and place it on the shelf.

Reading is lots of fun so read a book today. Tell your friends about this book and watch them read away.

Sing, sing, sing a book if you hear a song, sing the words loud enough and your friends might sing along.

As you read let your body keep time and move, rhythm is the best way to find your reading groove.

Teachers like to read books 'cause books are mind feeders, teachers are readers and readers are leaders and teachers will lead the way.

My sister is a good reader, she loves Harry Potter, so for her birthday we went shopping and books was all we got her.

Non-fiction are the books, that I like the best, full of details, full of facts, that usually are on tests.

Songs have words, words you read, rhythm leads the way, tap your foot, just keep time, as you read away.

When I want to read for fun, perhaps a little mystery, I grab a book from my school entitled American History.

LITTLE DITTIES ON WRITING

Writers write every day so they will get better, writers write everything: songs, and books, and letters.

Writers try to write their worst the first time through, the more they write the better they get and that is always true.

Writers write and readers read what the writers compose, comprehension is the goal, this everyone should know.

Our teacher wrote a poem for her cat named Critter, Critter didn't like the poem, so now it's kitty litter.

Kindergartners think it's cool to get a library card, once they master writing their name, writing's not that hard.

WE LIKE FROGS

(with Vermont kindergarten teachers)

> In our class
> We like frogs
> They can jump
> High and low
> Take the top off
> Of their cage
> And just let them go
> Hop—hop—hop
> Uhmmm, uhmmm, uhmmm.
>
> Frogs have tongues
> That stick out far.
> They can reach you
> Where you are.
> Frogs don't like
> To live in jars.
> So just let them go.
> Hop – hop – hop.
> Uhmmm, uhmmm, uhmmm.

 MUSICAL EXTENSIONS AND ACTIVITIES

How about a unit on frogs? Kids seem to love them. Here are some questions to use when getting your students ready to write about frogs. After the students have done their research, I encourage them to pretend that they are frogs on land for the first time, and try to get them to write a narrative song about how they'd spend their time, what food they'd look for, and how they might hide from danger.

Some Questions to Answer When Researching Frogs

- Make a list of words that describe frogs and their actions. Don't forget the verbs.

- Are frogs found all over the world? On a map of the world, mark all of the countries where frogs are found. What is the largest frog in the world? Where is it found? How big is it? What is the smallest frog in the world? Where is it found? How small is it?

- Do frogs live on land or water? Where else do they live? What does the word "amphibian" mean?

- How do frogs catch their food? What do they usually eat?

- How long does it take for a frog to flick out and retract its long, sticky tongue?

- How old can frogs live to be? What enemies do frogs have?

- Why do frogs blink their eyes when they swallow?

- Are all frogs good jumpers? What makes frogs able to jump so well?

- What do frogs do when they sense danger? How do they protect themselves from danger?

- Are there any poisonous types of frogs? If so, what are they called and where are they found?

- How do tree frogs climb and stay in trees? Where do tree frogs sleep?

- Why do frogs sit on logs?

- What sound(s) do frogs make? Do they have a special sound when danger is sensed?

- Do frogs hibernate? If so when, where, and for how long? Do male and female frogs hibernate in the same area?

- Why are frog eggs covered in jelly? How many eggs does a female frog lay at one time? Will all the eggs develop into frogs? What is a polliwog? What are the basic stages of a frog's life?

- If you were a tadpole living in a stream or pond, what would you have to do every day to survive? What would you eat? What would happen to your tail as you turned into a frog?

- What is the difference between a frog and a toad?

- Can you think of any songs, stories or poems about frogs?

- Who are some famous frogs, either fictional or non-fictional?

- What are some wives' tales and legends about frogs? Do frogs really cause warts? If you kiss a frog will it turn into a prince?

- Have your class read books like Wendy Watson's *Frog Went A-Courting* and after reading (and singing!) them, have your class write scripts and turn them into plays. Update the song. Add more verses, add movement, and create scenery, backdrops and costumes.

Here are some sample frog songs that I have written, collaborated on with other writers, or collected. Enjoy!!

ELVIS T. FROG (with students from Cromer Elementary School in Flagstaff, Arizona)

I may be going out on a limb (or lily pad) here, but I believe most people like both frogs and Elvis. Years ago, at a school visit in Arizona, the two finally came together. This song may never win a Grammy, but your grammy may like it if you sing it to her. Here's a good example of a song that combines human traits with an animal character.

> With a slimy green body
> Hair in a wild, black curl
> Hangin' out in secret swamp
> With all the boys and girls
> On a cool moony night
> Rockin' the night away.
> In Viva, Swamp Vegas
> There lived a frog
> And Elvis T. Frog was his name.
>
> In Viva, Swamp Vegas,
> Ribbit, ribbit, ribbit.
> Rockin' the night away.
> In Viva, Swamp Vegas,
> Ribbit, ribbit, ribbit,
> Elvis T.'s come to play.
>
> Sneakin' up on dragon flies
> Black cape a-flappin'
> On his midnight shift.
> Sticky tongue a-snappin'
> On a cool moony night
> Elvis T.'s come to play.

In Viva, Swamp Vegas
There lived a frog
And Elvis T. Frog was his name.
Viva, Swamp Vegas.
Viva, Swamp Vegas,
Viva, Viva, Swamp Vegas.

ELVIS, HAS LEFT THE POND!!!!

(Can be sung to "Viva, Las Vegas")

I wrote the next song after reading the book *Life Story: Frog* by Michael Chinery. Getting your students to pattern songs after books they have read is a great way to reinforce the facts that they have learned.

THE GREEN, GREEN FROG

Green, green frog.
Hoppin' on a log.
When he was a baby
Was a swimmin' polliwog.
Hoppin' on a log
Is a green, green frog
When he was a baby
Was a swimmin' polliwog.

Now green, green frog
Sittin' on a log
Catchin' flies with his tongue
In a dirty, muddy bog.
Sittin' on a log
Is a green, green frog,
Catchin' flies with his tongue
In a dirty muddy bog.

Then green, green frog
Leaps from his log
To a green lily pad
In the dirty muddy bog.
Leaps from his log.
Green, green frog
To a green lily pad
In a dirty muddy bog.

IF YOU SIT BY ME

For years, I have been observing students of all ages make a mess of getting settled in their seats. If their teachers tell them to scoot all the way to the end of the row, they inevitably park their tushes in the first seat they reach. Other students have to climb over them or try to force them to move. There are always faces made, and names called, and tushes pushed by other tushes. I wrote this song to help remind everyone of the rules.

> If you sit by me, don't lean.
> Keep your hands to yourself,
> Don't be mean.
> Don't tickle or tease,
> But say "Excuse me," or "Please"
> If you wanna sit by me.
>
> If you sit by me, don't push.
> Don't wiggle in your seat
> With your tush.
> These seats are too small
> And you're hoggin' them all.
> If you wanna sit by me
> Please don't push,
> With your tush, the end, but—really,
> Bum-mer!
>
> If you sit by me, act your best.
> Be polite and listen.
> Don't be a pest.
> Let's be nice and be friends for life
> And I'm glad you're sittin' by me.

MUSICAL EXTENSIONS AND ACTIVITIES

- Teach the song to your students. Go over each verse. Have your students come up with movements, gestures, and facial expressions that bring meaning to the words.

- Lead your students in a discussion of rules, manners, and good etiquette for situations where large groups of people have to be close together (in assemblies, on the bus, in the hall, in class, on the playground, etc). Brainstorm a list of good behaviors and bad behaviors. Write songs that can be sung as reminders of the rules. Post the songs on the wall, and sing them each time your class is going to be in a large-group situation.

THE NEW THREE LITTLE PIGS

Sing-Along!
TRACK 10

I wrote this song with the help of the teachers that attended a graduate-level summer course on enhancing literacy through the arts at the University of Nebraska at Kearney. This is a modern day update on the old story and song. I usually sing it in a jazzy style.

Mama Pig said
"Pack your bags,
Find you a home
Where no one nags."

So three cool pigs
Went out one day
Looking for sticks,
Bricks and HAY!!!!!! (say like the word Hey!!!)

Before too long
The piggies found
Big Bad Wolf
Was a-hanging around.

Huffin' and a-puffin'
And a-struttin' his stuff
Big Bad Wolf
Thought he was tough.

Then Big Bad Wolf
Had a change of heart
'Cause in the end
The piggies got smart.

- Have your students read and study other folk tales, nursery rhymes, and stories. Encourage them to re-write these tales for modern times. Have them see if they can find any modernized fairy tales in the library. Compare the updates with the originals.

- Have students go to the library and see how many different versions of "The Three Little Pigs" they can find. Have them develop a history of the story and encourage them to make oral presentations to the rest of the class. The origins of a story are usually fascinating.

- Share old folk tales and nursery rhymes with your students (perhaps you can pick some of the stories that you remember from your childhood, or compile a list of your students' favorites). Ask them to make lists of what can be learned from these old tales and stories. Is it still important for kids to learn these lessons?

MY TEACHER RIDES A HARLEY

(with Brod Bagert)

Most people don't expect a school teacher (who is also a single parent) to be motorcycle owner, yet alone a Harley rider. If you have an open mind you'll of course know better. This song was written for one cool teacher who rides a Harley!

> Some teachers knit, some teachers sew,
> Some teachers make cookies out of cookie dough,
> But I got a teacher who can't sit still
> She's a motorcycle mamma looking for a thrill
> Down in the land of bluegrass and barley
> I got a teacher... who rides a Harley.
> Vaaaa Rooooooooooom!
> Va Rooom Rooom Rooom!
>
> Zooming through the back roads of Bowling Green Kentucky,
> Biking cross the nation feeling kind of lucky,
> Pounding the pavement... throttles open wide,
> Watch out kids! There ain't no place to hide,
> Down in the land of bluegrass and barley
> I got a teacher... who rides a Harley.
> Vaaaa Rooooooooooom!
> Va Rooom Rooom Rooom!
>
> She wears black leather looking slim and trim
> But folks say a teacher should be proper and prim
> (She) smiles and says, "I'm a real role model,
> (I) show my kids a life that lives on open throttle."
> Down in the land of bluegrass and barley
> I got a teacher... who rides a Harley.
> Vaaaa Rooooooooooom!
> Va Rooom Rooom Rooom!

MUSICAL EXTENSIONS AND ACTIVITIES

- Use this song as an intro to a unit about the history of teachers and schools. What were teachers like 100 years ago? 150 years ago? 30 years ago? How have schools and teachers changed through the years? How have schools remained the same? (Some of the research activities from "The Homework Blues" (page 65) can be used with this song as well.)

- This is a great song to use as a way to get into a discussion on stereotyping and generalizations. As I've mentioned, most folks probably don't think of teachers (especially women who are single parents) as motorcycle riders. Yet I know many women who love motorcycles.

- If you are brave, have your students write a song based on you, their own teacher. Do you have any secrets you can share with your students? Kids love hearing each other's songs about their teachers. Of course, you have to be willing to share information about yourself with your students. I believe that in order to truly bond with your students (and gain their trust), you have to open up your heart and show that you are human, too. Students often find it hard to believe that one day, not really all that long ago, you sat in a classroom just like they are doing now.

- Of course, this song can be used with the song "Different, Yet the Same" (page 72) to explore the individual differences and similarities that bring us together as a community in the classroom.

MAZI, MY BOY

This song is about a young boy who lives in the rainforest and who is afraid he may be losing his home. It can be sung call and response or in unison. It really sounds great with rhythm instruments, jungle sound effects created by students, and rainforest sounds from commercially produced CDs.

No tree's a puzzle
For Mazi, my boy,
He's a climber.
Dangling for hours,
Swinging limb to limb.
Bananas at his fingertips
High above the ground.
Mazi loves the jungle.
The jungle is his home.

Mazi loves the trees—
Shelter for the birds,
Keeper of all the leaves.

Mazi speaks no English,
But he loves the jungle
As he shakes his head
And climbs towards the sky.

I climb a tree.
You climb a tree.
Above that jungle floor—
Fast as you can.
Climb toward the sun.
Call out for Mazi.
He won't reply.
Mazi speaks no English,

But he has a tear in his eye.
Mazi loves the jungle.
The jungle is his home.
When the jungle's gone
Where will Mazi go?

No tree's a puzzle,
For Mazi, my boy,
He's a climber.

 ## MUSICAL EXTENSIONS AND ACTIVITIES

- Have students find books on the rainforest, such as Lynne Cherry's *The Great Kapok Tree*, which was an inspiration to me as I wrote "Mazi, My Boy." It's a wonderful book with a powerful (but not preachy) message. Remind your students that reading good writing is a necessary part of becoming good writers. Encourage your students to write songs, poems, chants, or stories based on the books they use to gather information on jungles and rainforests.

- Talk about why the rainforests are being destroyed, who is hurt by the devastation, and who is benefiting from the destruction.

- Using a globe, an atlas, or a huge map, have students find and mark where all of the rainforests in the world are located. What are some characteristics that all rainforests have in common? What are some of the differences?

- Have your students research the daily lives (including foods eaten, games played, types of housing, entertainment, education, family life, transportation used, rites of passage, languages spoken, technology used, etc.) of those who live in or near rainforests. Encourage your students to compare their lives with the lives of the children who live in rainforests.

- Learn what you, your class, your family, your school, and your town can do to help preserve the rainforests and stop the destruction. Are there products that you can buy that support the rainforests? Should you be avoiding other products because they contribute to the destruction? The internet can be a valuable research tool for this subject.

- Have your students find recordings of music from the rainforests. (Mickey Hart, the Grateful Dead's percussionist, has released some great field recordings from the rainforest, as well as his own percussion music that is appropriate for jungle moods.) Discuss what types of instruments are used in the native music. Where do the instruments come from? How are they made? What are the songs about? Have students compare it to the music that they listen to on a daily basis.

- Draw, paint, or create a jungle backdrop in your classroom. When possible, play music and sound effects in the background while students are reading and writing about the rainforests. It helps give the feel and the emotions of the rainforests. I often listen to appropriate music while writing, to help court the muse and develop rhythm.

- As follow-up to their research on the rainforests, have students write poems, songs or stories about what it would be like for them to live in a rainforest.

- See if your students can locate pen pals from a rainforest region. Help them brainstorm a list of questions that you would like to have answered. See "Leroy the Kitty" (page 68) for a discussion of pen pal activities.

- Students can write their own songs that celebrate the rainforests. Here's an example.

JUNGLE SONG (with second graders from the Frank School in Arizona)

This was written for an ESL class that was studying the rainforest. I got my info from *New View: Rain Forest* by Fiona MacDonald. We sang this to the song "Wheels on the Bus" and used lots of repetition.

> The jungle is clammy, hot, rainy & cloudy,
> Hot, rainy and cloudy (2xs)
> The jungle is clammy, hot, rainy & cloudy,
> Life in the tropical rain forest.
>
> Birds & animals live in four layers,
> Live in four layers (2xs)
> Birds & animals live in four layers,
> Of the tropical rain forest.
>
> The top of the jungle is the emergent layer,
> Is the emergent layer (2xs),
> The top of the jungle is the emergent layer,
> Where the King Vulture sits all day.
>
> One layer down is the canopy,
> Is the canopy (2xs),
> One layer down is the canopy,
> Where the Toucan lounges on fruit every day.
>
> The next layer down is the understory,
> Is the understory (2xs),
> The next layer down is the understory,
> Home of the red-eyed frog.
>
> The bottom layer, the forest floor,
> The forest floor (2xs),
> The bottom layer, the forest floor
> Lives the_____.

MUMMIES MADE IN EGYPT

Written after reading *Mummies Made in Egypt*, an excellent book by Aliki. I wrote this song for a school play, and to show how much fun non-fiction can be for songwriters!

That author named Aliki
She must be pretty sneaky.
She crept into the crypt.
Wrote herself a script.
She did a little work
Turned her script into a book.
Telling how those mummies were made. I want my mummy!

It's called *Mummies Made in Egypt*,
A Reading Rainbow Book.
It's got all kinds of pictures.
Some might make you sick.
Like removin' a brain
By pullin' it through the nose
With the body just a-lyin' there
Without no mummy clothes—iiiiiii-yeeeeeee!!!!!!!!
I want my mummy!

You see Aliki is no dummy
'Cause she went and asked her mummy
To unravel the mystery
Of Egypt's ancient history.
Her mummy gave a description
Of those old Egyptians.
They only had one wish:
Forever they would live.
That's why those mummies were made.

Mum-mi-fi-ca-tion
Was her explanation.
In this land of sand and palm
Egyptians learned how to embalm.
It took 70 days to mummify this way.
Drying out the bodies
So they wouldn't decay.

All bedecked in jewels
Those Egyptians were no fools.
(They) believed that when they died
They began a new life.
In cloth they were bound.
They would wrap it round and round.
In a coffin they were placed.
Eternity they faced.
That's how those mummies were made. I want my mummy!

History shows, we have techno-pop and be-bop,
Now we have hip-hop.
Finger snapper, toe tapper.
Egyptians were the very first wrappers.
They found a way
To live forever and a day.
Wrappin' all the way
So they wouldn't turn to clay.

That's why the mummies were made (3xs).

 ## MUSICAL EXTENSIONS AND ACTIVITIES

Have your students read Aliki's book and encourage them to
do additional research on mummies and on ancient Egypt.
Have them add more verses to the song.

- Play the song before introducing the book. After they have listened, ask your students to list all of the facts that they learned from the song. After the class has gone over the book, have your students get into small groups and do re-writes of the song based on facts they have learned from studying the book.

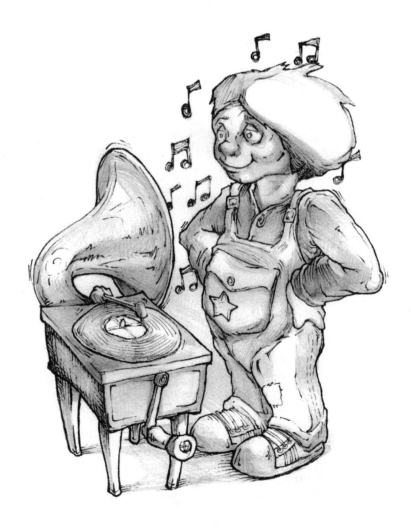

MY TEACHER THINKS HE'S ELVIS

This was written for a real principal who thinks he's Elvis, at least sometimes.

I walk into my classroom
On the first day of school.
I see all my friends
This year's gonna be cool.
From the corner of my eyes
Comes an incredible surprise.
I see my new teacher
In some strange disguise.

My teacher thinks he's Elvis,
Uh-huh, uh-huh, uh-huh.
My teacher thinks he's Elvis,
Uh-huh, uh-huh, uh-huh.
He's got a-long side burns.
He wears a-slicked back hair.
He wears blue sequin jumpsuits,
But we don't care.
My teacher thinks he's Elvis,
Uh-huh, uh-huh, uh-huh.
My teacher thinks he's Elvis
Uh-huh, uh-huh, uh-huh.
He's the teachin'est king of the school.

The first thing that he taught us
Were the rules of the school:
Always do your best,
To your friends, "Don't be cruel."
Keep up with your homework,
Come to school every day
Don't get "all shook up"
When things don't go your way.

Chorus

He teaches, uh-huh, uh-huh a-health,
A-readin' and writin' as such.
When I hand in my homework
He says, "A-thank you very much."
Hard work pays off.
Try to be a champ.
Set the world on fire.
Get your picture on a 29 cent stamp.

Chorus

I tell my parents
Teacher thinks he's the king.
But every time I tell them
They won't hear a thing.
During Parent Conference week
They'll finally see
When my teacher walks in
Dressed like Elvis Presley.

Chorus

 ## MUSICAL EXTENSIONS AND ACTIVITIES

- This song can be sung call and response, or with everyone singing in unison. Dance, movement, and drama can be added quite easily. I have seen several schools include this song in school plays, and in Poway, California, a group of parents created a great dance that they performed at my concerts. I have been told that this song works well for dance routines.

- Have students do some research as to what the United States (and the world in general) was like when Elvis began his career. Was he initially accepted? If not, why? What challenges did Elvis face when he was just starting out? Are there any bands today that are having trouble because of how they act or what they sing? How are their challenges similar to the challenges Elvis faced? Remember that when Elvis began his career media coverage was much different than it is today.

- A good book to share with your class is *History of American Bandstand: It's Got a Great Beat and You Can Dance to It* by Michael Shore with Dick Clark. This book has great photos and contains some great music history. It also includes the trends of the day: sayings, dances, commercials, foods, clothing, etc. Your students will love this.

- Elvis was not really known as a songwriter. He was really a "song interpreter" who sang most songs better than the original writers did. If possible find some of Elvis's recordings and the same songs by the original artists. Have your students make lists of how the recordings are similar and how they are different. This is a good introduction to a discussion on personal styles and influences. Elvis was influenced by country and the blues, and used those influences when interpreting bluegrass songs like "Blue Moon of Kentucky" by Bill Monroe in his own rockabilly style. Can your students point to specific influences on their own writing?

- Have your students interpret and perform each other's compositions, and discuss how the cover versions differ from the writer's original arrangement. The original author can learn a lot about their own work by hearing someone else's arrangement.

I WANT A GOOD BOOK TO READ

Ken Goodman's *What's Whole In Whole Language?* was the inspiration for this song. Some fifth and sixth grade students were asked to describe and explain in detail what the act of reading was and what readers are doing when they read. The students had some good ideas, but most were "stuck" and didn't know where to turn for help. I turned to Ken Goodman's book. Thank goodness I can read!

I want a good book to read
That's what I say.
I want a good book to read
Every day.
It's a real good habit
That's what I say.
I want a good book to read
Every day!

I like fiction, mysteries,
Poetry and prose.
Historical books
About people I should know.
Novels and non-fiction
And sports books, too.
There's always a book
For me and for you.

There are so many books
And it's so much fun.
So many great authors
I've barely begun.

Chorus

Comprehension of meaning
Is the goal of all readers.
I need to understand
What I just read.
So I use my prior learning
To gain the meaning of the text.

I predict, select, confirm,
And self-correct.
As I read I'm predicting
What happens in the text.
Then I monitor my reading
And I ask myself,
"Does it make sense?"

Chorus

When I find a word
I've never heard
I grab my dictionary
And expand my vocabulary.
And I soon find
A true reader's work
Is never done.

There are so many books
And it's so much fun.
So many new words
I've barely begun.

Chorus

And books will take me places
Where I've never been.
With books I can visit

Again and again.
Read 'bout other cultures
(And) how those people live.
I'll keep reading good books.
Books have so much to give.

Books describe emotions.
Books tell how people feel.
Sometimes I see myself
That's why books appeal.

Chorus

So find a good book
And read every day.
Exercise your mind
In a literary way.
Become the best reader
That you can be.
And when it comes to books –
You'll be a readin' VIP.

Chorus

 ## MUSICAL EXTENSIONS AND ACTIVITIES

- I learned how to read by singing the books I was trying to get
through. I have been asked many times to explain why I sang
books, how I came up with the idea, and if someone showed
me how to do it. All I can say is, it seemed natural to me.
This song is an exploration of how it happened and what the
process means to me. Here's another:

WHY SING A BOOK?

Why sing a book
You may ask yourself
Aren't books for reading
And sitting on a shelf?

That's much too limiting
I would say
A book should be sung
In a most lyrical way.

Let the words roll
Right off your tongue,
Yes, books are for reading
But some books can be sung.

BIBLIOGRAPHY

Aliki. *Mummies Made in Egypt*. New York: HarperTrophy, 1979.

Boyd, Jenny with Holly George-Warren. *Musicians in Tune: Seventy-Five Contemporary Musicians Discuss the Creative Process*. New York: Simon & Schuster, 1992.

Chenfeld, Mimi Brodsky. *Teaching Language Arts Creatively*. 2nd ed. San Diego: Harcourt, 1987.

Cherry, Lynne. *The Great Kapok Tree: A Tale of the Amazon Rain Forest*. New York: The Trumpet Club, 1990.

Chinery, Michael. *Life Story: Frog*. Mahwah, NJ: Troll Associates, 1991.

Copland, Aaron. *Music and Imagination*. Cambridge, MA: Harvard University Press, 1952.

Cox, Terry. *You Can Write Song Lyrics*. Cincinnati: Writer's Digest Books, 2000.

Davis, Sheila. *The Craft of Lyric Writing*. Cincinnati: Writer's Digest Books, 1985.

Gillette, Steve. *Songwriting and the Creative Process*. Bethlehem, PA: Sing Out!, 1995.

Goodman, Kenneth S. *What's Whole in Whole Language*. Toronto: Scholastic Lmtd., 1986.

Hirschhorn, Joel. *The Complete Idiot's Guide to Songwriting*. Indianapolis: Alpha, 2001.

Hughes, Langston. *The Book of Rhythms*. New York: Oxford USA, 1995.

Kotch, Laura and Leslie Zackman. *The Author Studies Handbook: Helping Students Build Powerful Connections to Literature*. New York: Scholastic Professional Books, 1996.

Lain, Sheryl. *A Poem for Every Student: Creating Community In A Public School Classroom*. Berkeley: National Writing Project, 1998.

Lieberman, Julie Lyonn. *You Are Your Instrument: The Definitive Musician's Guide To Practice and Performance*. New York: Huiksi Music Company, 1991.

MacDonald, Fiona. *New View: Rain Forest*. Austin: Raintree Steck-Vaughn, 1994.

Shore, Michael with Dick Clark. *History of American Bandstand: It's Got a Great Beat and You Can Dance to It*. New York: Ballantine Books, 1985.

Sloan, Carolyn. *Finding Your Voice: A Practical and Spiritual Approach to Singing and Living*. New York: Hyperion, 1999.

Strunk, Jr., William and E.B. White. *The Elements of Style*. 3rd ed. Boston: Allyn and Bacon, 1979.

Watson, Wendy. *Frog Went A-Courting*. New York: Lothrop, Lee & Shepard, 1990.

Winslow, Robert W. and Dallin, Leon. *Music Skills for Classroom Teachers*. Debuque: Wm. C. Brown Publishers, 1984.

Young, Sue. *The Scholastic Rhyming Dictionary*. New York: Scholastic, 1994.

ABOUT THE AUTHOR

Gary Dulabaum wears many hats: writer, songwriter, educator, child protection consultant, speaker, recording artist, musician, entertainer, and stand-up comedian. He says writing his first book was hard, but one of the most incredible learning experiences ever! He travels the United States sharing his love of music, rhythm, and using song as a teaching tool. He plays several instruments and lives in South Burlington, Vermont with his wife Anne-Marie Caron.

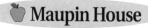